A Short Introduction to Judging and to Legal Reasoning

A Short Introduction to Judging and to Legal Reasoning

Geoffrey Samuel

Professor, Kent Law School, UK, and Professor affilié, École de droit, Sciences-Po, Paris, France

Edward Elgar
PUBLISHING

Cheltenham, UK • Northampton, MA, USA

Published by
Edward Elgar Publishing Limited
The Lypiatts
15 Lansdown Road
Cheltenham
Glos GL50 2JA
UK

Edward Elgar Publishing, Inc.
William Pratt House
9 Dewey Court
Northampton
Massachusetts 01060
USA

A catalogue record for this book
is available from the British Library

Library of Congress Control Number: 2016932484

This book is available electronically in the **Elgar**online
Law subject collection
DOI 10.4337/9781785365928

MIX
Paper from responsible sources
FSC® C013056
FSC www.fsc.org

ISBN 978 1 78536 591 1 (cased)
ISBN 978 1 78536 592 8 (eBook)

Typeset by Columns Design XML Ltd, Reading
Printed and bound in Great Britain by TJ International Ltd, Padstow

Contents

Preface

This relatively short book is designed as an independent work in itself and as a collection of cases and materials to complement both my *Rethinking Legal Reasoning* monograph (Edward Elgar, forthcoming) and my *A Short Introduction to the Common Law* (Edward Elgar, 2013). The cases and materials are linked by text in order that the book has a flow, and can thus be used as an independent introductory work; but this text will not venture into quite the same analytical depth as in the *Rethinking* work. In fact this present collection of materials, and the text that links them, grew out of a series of lectures delivered to first-year students at the Kent Law School in 2014. It should therefore be suitable for students who are starting out on their law programmes, as well as for students who would like to examine judging and legal reasoning in more depth.

Geoffrey Samuel
Kent Law School
June 2016

Acknowledgements

The author and publisher would like to thank the following publishers and individuals for their permission to quote from their works.

Brill NV
Cambridge University Press
Dalloz
Elsevier
Faber & Faber
Hart Publishing
IRJS Éditions
Oxford University Press
Presses Universitaires de France

The author would also like to thank the three anonymous referees for their very helpful comments and suggestions.

Table of cases and practice directions

Table of statutory texts

Introduction

The purpose of the chapters that follow is to look at the process of judging – how judges arrive at their decisions – and the kinds of reasoning that they employ in order to arrive at, or to support, these decisions. Judges in all European systems are obliged to state their reasons for their decisions and any failure to do this will normally be a ground in itself for appeal. There are, however, a range of complex issues that attach to judging and to legal reasoning. They can perhaps be summarised as a series of research questions:

- Are judges merely bureaucratic agents who mechanically apply the law or are they agents who have considerable freedom in resolving disputes that come before them?
- What kinds of reasoning processes are acceptable in judging and in arriving at a decision in a legal case?
- Are the judging and reasoning processes used by practising lawyers and judges themselves governed by legal norms or rules?
- Do judges in appeal courts judge and reason in exactly the same way as judges in first instance courts? Should they judge in the same way?
- When analysing the judging and reasoning processes used by practitioners and judges, can one distinguish between an 'internal' view (the view of those acting within the discipline of law) and an 'external' view (the view of those from another discipline looking at these legal reasoning processes)?
- Can one distinguish between – to use a dichotomy created by the jurist Mitchel Lasser (Lasser, 2004) – an 'official portrait' of judging and reasoning and an 'unofficial portrait'?
- To what extent is judging and legal reasoning guided or influenced by particular theories about law and legal knowledge?
- To what extent is knowledge about judging and legal reasoning to be gained by asking, and investigating, what legal reasoning has been (a diachronic approach)?
- To what extent is judging and legal reasoning influenced by the gender and social conditioning of the judge?

- Is it helpful to compare the reasoning employed by lawyers and judges with reasoning used by those in other disciplines (for example medics, natural scientists, film and literary critics)?
- To what extent is judging a matter of how one views the facts of a litigation dispute?
- What are the precise roles played by the standard reasoning techniques of induction, deduction and analogy?
- Are some reasoning methods (eg 'top-down' reasoning) illegitimate (at least in the common law tradition)?
- What role do concepts such as legal personality, ownership, contract, fault and damage play in legal reasoning?
- What role do metaphors play in judging and in legal reasoning?
- What role do legal and non-legal academics play in judging and in legal reasoning?
- Would it (or will it ever) be possible to produce an Artificial Intelligence (AI) programme that would permit a computer to judge and to reason just like a human judge?

These questions are by no means exhaustive. Indeed one purpose of these chapters is to provoke yet further questions about judging and legal reasoning. However, the questions hopefully give expression to most of the major issues associated with judging and reasoning in law.

Not all of these questions will be covered (or even tackled) in the chapters that follow, but some of the more important issues will be raised and discussed (or at least touched upon). The general approach that will be adopted is one based upon a metaphorical distinction employed by Professor Mitchel Lasser in his examination of legal reasoning in France (Lasser, 2004). He sees in France what he calls an 'official portrait' of judicial reasoning and an 'unofficial portrait'. This is, arguably, a useful distinction in that it gives expression, on the one hand, to a formalism that has an important political resonance given the history of judges and judging in France and, on the other hand, to a reality that even most judges might well recognise. The idea of an 'unofficial portrait' also permits one to go beyond the discipline of law itself and allow for a view of judging and legal reasoning from a social science and even a literary and film theory perspective. Of course, the object of the portraits in these chapters will not be the French legal tradition, although references to continental jurists and reasoning methods will be made. The object will be judging and reasoning in the common law jurisdictions, the main emphasis being on English law. However it must always be borne in mind that judging and reasoning within a discipline of 'law' (*ius*) has a very long tradition in Europe in general and it would be idle to think that English judges and jurists have been completely isolated from this wider historical tradition.

1. What judging and legal reasoning have been

One way of understanding judging, and the reasoning associated with it, is to ask what it has been. In posing this question with respect to law within what might be called the Western Tradition – that is the tradition that originated in Europe before spreading via colonialism to other parts of the world – one is faced with two sub-traditions, namely the civil law and the common law. The history of the common law in England is not one associated with Roman law texts or with Romano-Canonical procedure and so there are important differences with respect to the reasoning methods associated with the two traditions. However, particularly from the 19th century, there have also been interactions. Some have argued that although Roman law and common law had no genealogical connection, Roman jurists and common lawyers share some of the same casuistic (or 'bottom up') methods. Jurists from both legal systems tended and tend to reason from practical cases. Looking at what legal reasoning has been in the civil law is, therefore, of some relevance.

1.1 ROMAN LEGAL REASONING

The starting point for reasoning for much of Roman law's history was whether or not a person had a legal action (*actio*).

Digest of Justinian Book 9 Title 2 (translation Geoffrey Samuel)

52. ALFENUS, *Digest, book 2* ... 2. On Capitoline hill mules were pulling two loaded wagons; the drivers of the first wagon which had tilted up were supporting it so as to make it easier for the mules to pull it; however while doing this the first cart started to roll backwards and when the drivers, who had been between the two wagons, had got out of the way, the rear cart was hit by the one in front and moved back and crushed someone or other's slave boy. The owner of the slave boy asked me against whom he should claim. I replied that the law was to be found in the facts of the case (*respondi in causa ius esse positum*). For if the drivers who were supporting the wagon got themselves out of the way on their own accord and it was as a result of this fact that the mules were not able to hold the wagon and were themselves dragged back by the load, then no

action could be brought against the owner of the mules. However with respect to the men who were holding up the tilted wagon a claim under the *lex Aquilia* could be brought; for it is no less the doing of damage he who voluntarily lets go of something he is holding up so that it hits something; for example if someone who steers an ass does not restrain it, he would do wrongful damage in the same way as if he had discharged a spear or anything else from his hand. But if the mules behaved in the way they did because they were frightened by something, and the drivers left the wagon fearing they would be crushed, while no action could be brought against the men, an action could be brought against the owner of the mules. However if neither mules nor men were the cause, but the mules could not hold up the weight, or while trying slipped and fell and the wagon went backwards and the men had been unable to bear the weight of it when the wagon tilted over, neither the owner of the mules nor the men would be open to an action. What is indeed certain, whatever the situation in this affair, is that no claim could be made against the owner of the mules pulling the wagon behind, for they did not go back on their own accord but because they were hit and pushed backwards.

One might note here how the jurist reasons 'bottom up' so to speak. In order to determine whether the claimant has an action one must examine in detail the circumstances: the law is to be found in the facts (*in causa ius esse positum*). The Romans thus placed great emphasis on factual examples; they moved from one factual situation to another. The jurists also frequently quoted other jurists, either in agreeing with them or perhaps suggesting a different result from the facts.

Digest of Justinian Book 8 Title 5 (translation Geoffrey Samuel)

8. ULPIAN, *Edict, book 17* ... 5. Aristo says in an opinion given to Cerellius Vitalis that he does not think that smoke can in law be discharged from a cheese workshop on to the buildings above it, unless the buildings are subject to a servitude of such a kind and this is admitted. The same author says that it is not legal for water or anything else to be discharged from the building above to the one below: as a man is lawfully able to do things in his own premises only when he discharges nothing onto those of another; now smoke like water is something that can be discharged. An action is given in this case against the upper owner as well as the lower owner not to act in this way. He says finally that Alfensus writes that an action can be brought in which it is asserted that a person cannot lawfully cut stone on his own land in such a way that fragments fall onto my land. Aristo thus says that a person who has hired a cheese workshop from the town of Minturnæ can be prevented from discharging smoke by the owner of the upper floor, but he would have an action against Minturnæ on the contract of hire; he adds that one can bring an action against the person who discharges the smoke in saying that he has no lawful authority (*ius ei non esse fumum immittere*) to discharge smoke. It must follow, in contrast, that one can bring an action to assert that he has lawful authority to discharge smoke (*ius esse fumum immittere*); this also appears to have Aristo's approval. And indeed an interdict *uti*

possidetis can be obtained if one is prevented from doing what he wants on his own land. 6. A doubt is raised by Pomponius in his Readings (*Lectiones 41*) as to whether one can bring an action to assert lawful or non-lawful discharge of smoke that is not serious, for example smoke from a hearth. And the major view is that one cannot bring an action, just as one cannot bring an action to assert that it is lawful to light a fire or sit down or to wash on one's own land.

Again one can see how important the legal action (*actio*) or (to use today's language, remedy) was in Roman legal analysis. This is the 'institutional' viewpoint from which the facts are set out and analysed. One can thus describe the method as being remedy orientated. The jurists are not starting out by quoting 'the law' in terms of some pre-existing set or rules of 'rights'. They are basically asking whether or not the claimant has an action. However the Romans did write introductory textbooks (*institutiones*) for students and these texts differ from the great practitioner work of the *Digest of Justinian*.

Gaius, *Institutes*, Book IV (translation Geoffrey Samuel)

1. It remains to speak of actions. And if we ask what *genera* of actions there are, it seems in truth to be two, *in rem* and *in personam*. For those who have spoken of four in counting *sponsionum* in the class of *genera* they have treated a species of action as if it is generic. 2. An action *in personam* is one where we sue someone obligated to us either in contract (*ex contractu*) or in delict (*ex delicto*), that is where we claim that he ought 'to convey (*dare*), to do (*facere*) or to perform (*praestare*)' something. 3. An action *in rem* is one where we claim either a corporeal thing to be ours or some *ius* [in a thing], as for instance the *ius* of using or usufruct, going over, driving over or conducting water over land or of raising the height of a building or of having an unobstructed view. A negative opposing action [*in rem*] is available to the adversary. 4. And so having described actions, it is clear that it is not possible for us to claim our thing from another in the following way: 'if it appears it ought to be conveyed'. For what is ours (*quod nostrum est*) cannot be conveyed to us since of course to be conveyed is to be understood as what is given to us is made ours but a thing which is already ours cannot be made more ours. It is true that one's hatred of thieves, in order to multiply the actions for which they are liable, it has become accepted that, in addition to the penalty of double or quadruple, thieves are even liable for the recovery of a thing set out in this way: 'if it appears that they ought to convey', although this action for what is ours is available against them as well. 5. Actions *in rem* are, on the one hand, called vindications (*vindicationes*); actions *in personam*, on the other hand, whereby we claim that someone ought to convey or do, are called *condictiones*. 6. Sometimes we sue in order only to obtain our thing (*res*), in others only to obtain a penalty, and in others to obtain our thing and a penalty. 7. We sue only for a thing in for example in actions founded on a contract (*ex contractu*). 8. We sue for a penalty in actions for theft and insult and,

according to some, for the action for aggravated robbery; for in this situation both the *vindicatio* and the *condictio* are open to us. ...

Here, again, one can see just how important actions were to the Roman jurists up to the end of the Classical period (middle of the 3rd century AD). However this text is far more general and begins to read a little like a book of rules, although Gaius probably did not regard his *Institutes* as being about stating rules (*regulae*). One particular, important technique employed in this textbook should be noted: namely the importance of classification according to genus and species. Some regard this development of classification techniques (which started a century before Gaius) as the foundation of a legal 'science'. As for the whole of law, Gaius classified it in the following way:

Gaius, *Institutes*, Book I

8. All law that we use relates either to persons (*persona*), or to things (*res*) or to actions (*actiones*).

This is basically the classification scheme that remains dominant in modern European law, although the category of actions has been replaced by 'obligations'. It is one of the first examples of a structural approach whose coherence is such that the scheme amounts to a system (see 5.5).

1.2 MEDIEVAL JURISTS

At the end of the Roman Empire a huge collection of Roman law, compiled under the authority of the emperor Justinian, was published in 533 AD. The central part of this *Corpus Iuris Civilis* was the *Digest*, which consisted of extracts from the many law books which had been written largely from the century before Christ up until the 3rd century AD. This *Digest* collection of Roman law was rediscovered in the 11th century and became the basis of law teaching in Italian and, later, French universities. The later medieval jurists wrote long commentaries on every part of the *Corpus Iuris*.

Bartolus, Interpretum Iuris Civilis Coryphaei, in *Ius Universum Civile, Commentaria*, Basileae, Froben, 1562, p 463 (translation Geoffrey Samuel)

When the owner of a lower tenement lights a fire in the course of normal family life this is, then, lawful and he will not be held liable if the smoke ascends unless he does it with a wrongful intent. And in the same way if the owner of the upper tenement allows water to flow, for his water time piece, he will not be liable if the water descends unless he was doing it with wrongful intent. But if the owner of the lower tenement was running a shop or an inn, where he was continually having a fire which generated a large amount of smoke, this is not lawful (*non licet*) according to him [Aristo]. In the same way if the owner of the upper tenement allows water to flow beyond the normal amount this is unlawful he [Aristo] says.

This commentary is taken from a late medieval Roman law specialist who was commenting upon the Ulpian text set out earlier (see 1.1). What is important to notice here is that Bartolus (1313–1357) is adopting a different viewpoint. He is not approaching the problem in terms of whether or not an action or remedy is available; he is, instead, analysing the facts from the position of whether or not it is lawful to make smoke. He also introduces into the analysis something not really mentioned by Ulpian, namely fault. Ulpian does not discuss in the actual cheese shop text what the position would be if someone made smoke in order intentionally to annoy a neighbour. However elsewhere in the *Digest* of Roman law there are texts dealing with damage wrongfully caused and, of course, Bartolus, who knew by heart the whole of Roman law, would be well aware of these other texts. Thus he is in effect bringing together in one text what the Romans had dealt with in a mass of separate texts. Moreover Bartolus is applying a particular method called a dialectical analysis. This is where a problem and (or) a text is analysed in terms of an either/or (*aut* ... *aut* in Latin) scheme. It is in essence the basis of what today we call an algorithm, which can be set out as shown in Figure 1.1.

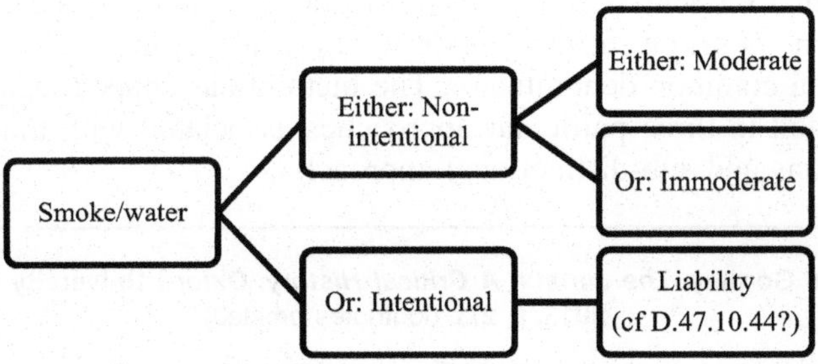

Figure 1.1 Bartolus and the cheese shop

One important characteristic of this method is the exclusion of any third way.

> **Ian Maclean, *Interpretation and Meaning in the Renaissance*, Cambridge University Press, 1992, p 39** (footnotes omitted)
>
> … Renaissance jurisprudence is to be distinguished from medicine by its predilection for the *species contraria immediata* of opposition; persons are masculine or feminine, guilty or not guilty, persons, things and actions are in a given category or are not, words are used literally or figuratively; there is no third term or coexistence of possibilities. The authoritative and logical summaries of points in commentary and monograph encourage this decisiveness, which lawyers see as a distinguishing mark of their art.

Such a scholastic approach might seem somewhat pedantic today, but the development of this method was in its time revolutionary.

> **Walter Ullmann, *Law and Politics in the Middle Ages,* Sources of Legal History, 1975, p 87**
>
> The scholastic method was dialectics brought to perfection: it was a method by which numerous contradictions in the *Corpus* of law were to be solved by the mental operation of a distinction and if necessary subdistinctions and subdivisions, until a common denominator of the contradictory passages could be found. This resulted in the complicated and finely woven texture of numerous distinctions which makes it so difficult for the modern reader to penetrate into the matrix of medieval governmental ideas profitably. Within civilian jurisprudence the distinctive feature of this method was the triad consisting of the *positio* (one standpoint or one interpretation or one legal enactment) contradicted by the *oppositio* and the *solutio* which deduced the elements which were common to both the *positio* and *oppositio*. It was this method which the civilian (and canonistic) glossators practised in the twelfth century.

This is an excellent description of the dialectical (scholastic) method, although it might be more accurate to say that one induced (rather than deduced) a common denominator. The method has shaped legal thinking and resulted in three particular approaches associated with this casuistic (distinctions and sub-distinctions) approach.

> **James Gordley, *The Jurists: A Critical History*, Oxford University Press, 2013, p 277** (footnotes omitted)
>
> The problem of applying authoritative texts to situations that they do not expressly cover is one that modern lawyers face as well. The medieval jurists

found ways of doing so that modern lawyers still use. One is to generalize a text that deals with one situation so that it can be applied to others. Another is to limit a text framed in general terms by distinguishing situations to which it should be applied from those to which it should not. The third way is to move directly and by analogy from the situations dealt with expressly in the texts to a different situation. Modern jurists proceed in these ways when they apply a code, a statute, or a precedent. Since the task is similar, this similarity is not surprising. Beginning with an authoritative text, one can move up, down or sideways. These are the only directions in which one can move.

A good example of the second method outlined by Professor Gordley is to be found in the case of *Birmingham CC v Oakley* (2001) (see 2.4). These outlined methods are, then, still in use today but, as Gordley later points out, modern jurists use other methods as well (Gordley, 2013, 42).

1.3 LATER JURISTS

In the 16th century there were further changes in the style and method of legal reasoning.

Geoffrey Samuel, Legal Reasoning and Argumentation, in James D Wright (editor-in-chief), *International Encyclopedia of the Social & Behavioral Sciences*, 2nd edition, 2015, Vol 13, Elsevier, 776, pp 778–779

… [a]lthough the Roman texts, and the practical problems discussed by the Roman jurists, were large and extensive, they did not cover everything and so the medieval jurists were faced with the problem of applying these texts to new situations. They did this in a largely casuistic way; they started out at the level of fact – persons and things – and developed Roman law notions using induction and analogy. Thus they might generalise a text by way of induction so that the rule (*regula*) could be applied to the new situation or they might take a particular factual problem discussed in the Roman texts and apply it by way of analogy (Gordley, 2013, 33–45). Equally they limited the application of a text or a rule by the use of distinctions and dialectical oppositions (Ullmann, 1975, 87). In doing this the later medieval jurists – the Commentators – fashioned what might be termed an algorithmic approach to legal reasoning and problem-solving (*aut … aut*: either … or). …

When one looks forwards from the medieval jurists a very different reasoning model gradually emerges. The change came in the 16th century with a school of French jurists known as the Humanists who developed a new approach towards the Roman texts (see generally Kelley, 1970). The humanists sought, on the basis of Roman classical law, to establish law as a science through which it could be explained clearly and systematically (Stein, 1999, 79–82). They wanted to cut through all the old 'pedantic' glosses and casuistic reasoning of the past – to get back to the original Roman texts and intentions of the authors who wrote them – so that the law could be perceived as a coherent whole. The emphasis henceforth was no longer to be on the particularities of the case and its analysis through dialectical distinctions and analogies but on what might be called the 'architecture' of the legal system – on how it fitted together as an interrelating systematic whole (Thireau, 2001, 232–238; Villey, 2006, 454–487).

Despite the fact that the humanist project had, at the time, little influence on legal practice or the methods employed by practitioners – the *Mos Italicus* (late medieval Italian methods) continued to dominate practice right into the 17th century (Jones, 1940, 34–35) – the longer term effect of this humanist revolution on legal reasoning proved immense. During the 17th and 18th centuries attention turned away from the kind of casuistic methods that characterised the Roman and medieval jurists towards a deductive and then axiomatic approach to reasoning. The authority of texts, which was the basic epistemological paradigm of the medieval age, gave way to a new paradigm, namely the authority of coherence. Thanks to jurists who were also mathematicians, such as Wilhelm Leibniz (1646–1716) and Christian Wolff (1679–1754), legal reasoning became associated with geometry (*mos geometricus*); solutions to legal cases were, accordingly, to be solved uniquely by the use of deductive logic (Gordley, 2013, 165–194; Champeil-Desplats, 2014, 60–63). The result was a complete change in the nature and style of law books. The dialectical method of division, distinction, induction and analogy, rooted in practical case examples, was replaced by a highly systematised set of ever more abstract legal propositions that no longer followed the order set out in the main source of Roman law itself, namely the *Digest*. They adopted the style and structure which characterised the *Institutes*. Thus, in France, the jurist Jean Domat (1625–1696) rearranged Roman law in its 'natural order' so that the Roman law was to be learned and applied, not through the reading and application of the original texts, but through a set of principles. The great advantage that this textbook reform brought to law – an advantage for practitioners as well as students – was that the law (in effect Roman law) became very much easier to read and absorb (Gordley, 2013, 145).
…

Sir Henry Maine said that the 16th and 17th centuries were a great juridical era but that reform of the law consisted of reform of the law books (Maine, 1890, 363). What did he mean? The medieval jurists, in their commentaries on the *Digest*, religiously followed the order of this Roman work, which, unlike the *Institutes*, was not based on any coherent plan. However the Humanist jurist Hugues Doneau (1527–1591) re-thought the whole of the *Digest* in the new way.

Hugues Doneau, *Commentarii de Jure Civili*, 6th German re-edition (1822), Book 1, Chapter 1 (first published 1596) (translation Geoffrey Samuel)

§ 2. Why I so feel the need to warn you at this early stage [about the order and arrangement of the *Digest*] I will set out briefly. With the civil law, which is the part of the law which assigns each person their rights, prescribes as it were things in two parts, and it is this order upon which we will focus; what rights each person is recognised as having, and the rationality of this recognition, in order that they can be dealt with later in much more depth in their own section. There is nothing perverse in the *Digest* and what relates to each of the two parts will be collected together and explained. For the right that each person has is partly in the person himself and partly in an external thing. However the rational determination of our right involves examining legal proceedings. How, I ask, can this right and rational way of knowing our rights be contrary to the way its various parts are instituted by the compilers? This is because you find set out the rights of personal status of some people in a few words followed by the division of things, and then is set out that part which is concerned with judges, jurisdiction, the right to summon to court, and things preceding the judgment, and the stages up to the decision. Why? So that our judgments are properly known. And from where actions, as much *in rem* as *in personam*, are immediately afterwards the subject of treatment. Therefore from judgments our right is obtained through rational reasoning, informing us clearly beforehand what is our right, what we can deduce from a judgment, what they should have taught us. Instituting a claim, given that everything is a matter of our right, our debts, we will understand beforehand what these are. And so then knowledge of what each person's right is, is something that by its very nature ought to precede any claim; this being known how, it might be asked, is the means of obtaining it.

§ 3. Does one go about explaining each part one by one? Indeed, so that each part of the limbs of the body are exposed; but only the limbs are discoverable, often scattered around and distant from the head, rather than the body itself. First, the question of rights regarding the status of persons is raised and what fixed rights that almost every person he himself has; these are life (*vita*), bodily integrity (*corporis incolumitas*), liberty (*libertas*) and reputation (*existimatio*). ...

Doneau set out his commentaries according to the plan of the *Institutes of Justinian* (that is the plan inherited from the *Institutes of Gaius*) and from the position, not of different kinds of action (*actio*), but of 'rights' (*ius*). He rethought Roman law from the position, first, of what rights each person has as a person (law of persons) and, secondly, what rights each person has in external things (law of things). With regard to the former – the law of persons – he said that these rights were life, bodily integrity, liberty and reputation. With regard to the latter – the law of things – he saw these rights as being divided into two kinds, namely 'what is ours' (law of property) and 'what is owed to us' (law of obligations). He thus established the legal plan to be found underpinning all of the modern civil codes; private law is sub-divided into persons, property and obligations. Doneau's use of the institutional plan was taken up by other writers, in particular the 18th-century French jurist – said to be the father of the French *Code civil* – Robert Pothier (1699–1772).

Robert Joseph Pothier, *Pandectis Justinianeis in Novum Ordinem Redactis, De Diversis Regulis Juris Antiqui*, Volume I, Pisis, 1825 edition, pp 5–6 (translation Geoffrey Samuel)

This work will be divided into five parts.

In the first part are offered the general rules of law either natural or civil, that is to say which cannot be said to be special to a particular part of the law, and then those which belong to the leading notions of the laws and also their interpretation.

The second part will contain those regarding persons.

The third regarding things.

The fourth regarding actions, or judgments, the order of judgments etc.

These three objects are the universal objects of private law, For 'all law that we use pertains to persons, to things or to actions' (J.1.2.12).

The fifth part contains public law.

To return to Doneau, one might note also how he was the first to identify what today we would call 'human rights'. As for the law of actions, this he regarded as something separate from substantive law and which belonged to the law of procedure. Doneau, in short, is the true grandfather of the modern civil law. Doneau did not, however, reduce the content of the *Digest* to an *Institutes*-length book. Quite the opposite since his *Commentarii* runs to 28 volumes. It was the French jurist Jean Domat (1625–1696) who reduced Roman law to a somewhat shorter work.

J Domat, *Les loix civiles dans leur ordre naturel* (2nd ed, 1695; nouvelle édition 1735) (with references), Preface (translation Geoffrey Samuel)

It seems very strange that the Civil Laws, whose usage is so necessary, be so little known, and that being nearly all about rules of equity, knowledge of which is to us natural, of which the study ought to be equally easy and agreeable, are so difficult and so painstaking.

However it must be recognised that the manner by which these laws are collected in the Books of Roman Law, which are the only source of these laws, makes it not at all easy to understand. And it is this which, among those whose profession obliges them to know these laws, results in some who do not know them, and that no one can become well versed except by a long and painstaking study.

Domat achieved this reduction by re-presenting Roman law as a series of easily understandable propositions. Take for example the cheese shop problem discussed by Ulpian (D.8.5.8.5: above 1.1).

J Domat, *Les loix civiles dans leur ordre naturel* (2nd ed, 1695; nouvelle édition 1735) (with references), First Part, Book I, Title XII, Section XII (translation Geoffrey Samuel)

X. Works and other things that each person can do or have in his own house and which spread into the apartments of those who have a part of the same building, or neighbour's houses, or unpleasant smells such as from tanners and dyers, and other different discomforts a neighbour can cause to another, must be suffered if a servitude is established. And if there is no servitude, the discomfort will be either suffered or prevented, according to the quality of the area, and the discomforts itself, and according to the rules of the police or of usage, if there are any, that will apply to the situation (D.8.5).

Gone is the casuistic case approach based upon the availability of a legal action; law is now a matter of abstract principles which read more like extracts from the final title of the *Digest*, namely *de regulis iuris* (on rules of law) (D.50.17).

1.4 LEGAL REASONING IN THE LATER CIVIL LAW

This reduction to a set of *regulae* had an important effect on legal reasoning in that the propositions came to be regarded as 'axioms' (*axiomata*).

Joham Gottlieb Heineccius, *Elementa Juris Civilis Secundum Ordinem Pandectarum*, 1785 edition, Book 9, Title 2, Lex Aquilia (translation Geoffrey Samuel)

§ 183 From these definitions are the following axioms: I. Whenever there is malice or negligence and damage there is an action based on the lex Aquilia. II. This statute requires that through our physical things being damaged by a physical act our patrimony is diminished.

§ 184 Since, then, it is at least negligence or malice that the lex Aquilia requires, the consequence is 1) that any negligence, even the slightest is sufficient (D.9.2.44pr). 2) Anyone intervening is obliged to show diligence otherwise he commits wrongful damage whether directly or by omission (D.9.2.8pr). 3) And so this includes inexperience and 4) weakness, if it would arise from inexperience, or from his own weakness if it would be a danger to others (D.9.2.8.1).

§ 185 Thence we infer 5) no action is possible against someone not guilty of negligence, such as a madman or a young infant if still baby-like and does not know what he is doing (D.9.2.5.2). 6) in neither case can it be imputed (D.9.2.5.3) and moreover it is not 7) damage to another without wrongfulness occurring from someone who can legally use it. Which at first is moderate and irreproachable relating to someone in guardianship, which becomes an aggressive unjust violent force threatening life or danger to one's body which if continued would kill the person in guardianship.

One can compare this text with D.9.2.52.2 (see 1.1). Legal reasoning is no longer about practical cases, but about high-level 'axiomatic' rules. The legal reasoner does not start out from facts but from the rule. The method is one of logical deduction with the judge being considered little more than a 'machine' mechanically applying the law to facts that have been fed to the court. By the 19th century the whole of fault liability had been reduced to a single axiom.

***Code civil* 1804**

Art 1382 [now art 1240]. Any act whatsoever by a person which causes damage to another obliges the person by whose fault it has occurred to repair it.

Concepts equally lay at the basis of this 'axiomatic' reasoning. For example, in Roman law the whole of the law of property was focused around three basic concepts: ownership (*dominium*, *proprietas*), possession (*possessio*) and rights in another's property (*ius*). However, as we have seen, the Romans did not reason by starting out from abstract definitions of these concepts, for all definitions are dangerous said a Roman jurist (D.50.17.202) and, anyway, the law was not to be found in abstract rules (D.50.17.1). Indeed, there is no definition of ownership to be found anywhere in the Roman sources. It was the medieval jurist Bartolus (building on the work of earlier medieval jurists) who induced out of all the Roman texts a definition.

Bartolus, *In primam Digesti Novi partem Commentaria*, ad D.42.2.17.1 nos 4 and 5 (translation Geoffrey Samuel)

What then is ownership? My reply is that it is the right (*ius*) in a physical thing of complete disposal unless legislation prohibits it ... Why do I say complete disposal? Because of [C.4.35.21] and because it is differentiated from possession, which is the right to stand on a thing (*ius insistendi rei*). ...

I ask, how many kinds of ownership exist? Some doctor from Orleans, as recounted by that German doctor who held a repetition here yesterday, says there is only one type of ownership. But there are two. And I prove this in referring to *l. possessores in fin C. de fundis patrimonialibus lib. 11* [C.11.62.12.1] where it is said that a person who holds land in long title (*emphyteuta*) is owner.

> And yet another remains owner, that is to say the lessor (*concedens*) [C.4.66.1-2]. And if there are two owners there are two forms of ownership because the same ownership cannot be split between two persons as stated in [D.13.6.5.15].
> ...

This definition, much later, became an axiom.

> **Joham Gottlieb Heineccius, *Elementa Juris Civilis Secundum Ordinem Pandectarum*, 1785, Book 41, 1, De Adquirendo Rerum Domino**
> (translation Geoffrey Samuel)
>
> **§ 161** Ownership is a right in a corporeal thing from which flows the ability to dispose of it and the right to vindicate it, unless statute, agreement or a voluntary will provision opposes it. Where this ability to dispose and to vindicate come together in the same person, so that both can be enjoyed *in solidum*, this is called FULL ownership; where it is split between two, so that one person's full interest to use of the thing can be vindicated as a right while the other person has the ability to dispose of the thing this is LESS than full ownership (*minus plenum*). And here *UTILE* and *DIRECTUM* are divided.

Despite writing in the early 18th century, Heineccius cannot escape the influence of the medieval jurists. His distinction between the two types of ownership was not actually to be found in Roman law – although a person who held land under a long lease, although not owner, was finally given an *actio in rem* (D.6.3.1.1) – but was an invention of the medieval jurists who were trying to apply Roman law to their feudal society. In fact the French jurists of the 17th century abandoned this dichotomy. Consequently by the time of codification there was just a single form of ownership.

> ***Code civil* (1804)**
>
> **Art. 544** Ownership (*la propriété*) is the right to enjoy and to dispose of things in the most absolute manner, provided that one does not make a usage prohibited by legislation or by regulations.

One often says that this definition of ownership is Roman in origin. Certainly in spirit it is Roman. But the definition is the result of the reasoning on Roman law by subsequent jurists. It indicates just how important jurists such as Bartolus were in shaping our modern view of the civil law.

When one turns to possession the Romans did get closer to formulating something of a definition. Or, at least, they formulated certain conditions.

Digest of Justinian Book 41 Title 2

3. PAUL, *Edict, book 54.* Possession is possible only of corporeal things. 1. And we obtain possession by physical act (*corpore*) and intention (*animo*), not by intention alone or by physical act alone. But when we say physical act and intention are required to obtain possession it is certainly not to be taken to mean that that he who wants to possess an estate must walk around the whole of the land; it is sufficient to enter any part of the estate while having the intention and purpose of possessing the whole of the land up to its boundary.

12. ULPIAN, *Edict, book 70* ... 1. Ownership (*proprietas*) has nothing in common with possession: and thus whosoever brings a *vindicatio* for the thing is not to be refused the interdict *uti possidetis* ...

17. ULPIAN, *Edict, book 76* ... 1. There is this difference between ownership (*dominium*) and possession, ownership nevertheless continues even when he does not wish it, possession however departs when he decides not to possess.

30. PAUL, *Sabinus, book 15.* Whosoever possesses a building as a whole, is not regarded as possessing the individual things in the building. The same must be said both of a ship and of a cupboard …

From these basic conditions a later civilian such as Heineccius was able to construct not just a whole deductive model of axioms but one that had the notion of a right (*ius*) at the basis of the property structure.

Joham Gottlieb Heineccius, *Elementa Juris Civilis Secundum Ordinem Pandectarum*, 1785, Book 41, Title 2, De Adquirendo vel Amittenda Possessione (translation Geoffrey Samuel)

§ 197 Having dealt with ownership, possession now follows. To possess is to have, hold or detain for a period of time. And the word is not meant as the place of standing but is meant as I can take over the place of standing. And so *POSSESSIO* in both its natural and grammatical sense is the bare detention of a thing (*nuda rei detentio*) without any right in the thing (*iure in re*). In the civil and legal sense, it is the detention of a corporal thing with the intention (*animus*) of having it.

§ 198 Who has this intention of having the thing thus has, provided that he believes that no one else is the owner, *BONAE FIDE* possession. If he does not believe that someone else is not the owner, it is said that he is a *MALAE FIDE* possessor. Thus non defective possession (*NON VITIOSA*) is where he possesses without force, stealth or permission of the owner (*nec vi, nec clam, nec precario*). Defective possession in contrast, is where there is such defectiveness present. Finally who has possession founded upon a just title has just (*IUSTA*) possession; who does not is said to have unjust (*INIUSTA*) possession.

§ 199 Thus possession is not a matter of law but fact. And so it seems to be a mistake to say that he who possesses has a real right (*ius in re*). It is thus a correct observation to say that a division into a right *in re* and a claim *ad rem* is not a relevant legal one in respect of possession.

§ 200 It is now easy to understand the axioms: I. Possession is acquired by physical act (*corpore*) and intention (*animo*) (D.41.2.3.1, 8, 51). II. Intention alone retains possession so that another person will not acquire it (D.41.2.3.7, 5, 30.5). III. Just as in the manner it is acquired, it is ordinarily lost (in the same way) (D.41.2.8, D.50.17.153). …

§ 202 From this same axiom we say 1) proper possession is possible of corporal things, and so 2) if it is of an incorporeal thing it is only quasi possession. 3) Possession applies only to things not to free people (D.41.2.23.2), although possession of people once acquired in good faith can be retained while the question of their freedom is being litigated. 4) One cannot acquire possession of some things, the commerce of men (D.41.2.30.1) for example who are dead and even less possession through them or things which are not in a state of being possessed (D.41.3.3.5).

§ 203 Finally from this first axiom it follows that 1) there is no possession of an inheritance even when all the rights to it are transferred unless it is physically taken (D.41.2.23pr, 30.5). 2) Any kind of physical taking will suffice or entering into land, and so neither 3) the whole of the land has to be walked all over (D.41.2.3.1, 48, 2), nor 4) is it unhelpful to see this as a fiction, as if accepting a key when assigning custody (*custodia*) of a thing (D.41.2.1.21, 51). Intention and title to possession ought to be present, and indeed the title must be true and not a mistaken one (D.41.2.34pr), nor 6) can anyone change for himself the title to possession (D.41.2.3.19, 19pr). …

One thus ends up with a single definition of possession in the form of an axiom.

***Code civil* 1804**

Art. 2228 Possession is the detention or the enjoyment of a thing or of a right that we hold or that we exercise ourselves or through another who holds it or who exercises it in our name.

One might note, however, that in this French definition one can possess not just a physical thing but also a right. Does this mean that one has the right (*ius possessionis*) to a right?

1.5 LEGAL FORMALISM (DOGMATICS)

The reasoning methods that attached to Roman law scholarship, particularly from the 16th century onwards, were to lead to what became known as legal formalism or, in the language of the civil law, legal dogmatics ('dogmatic' not being a pejorative expression in this sense).

Véronique Champeil-Desplats, *Méthodologies du droit et des sciences du droit*, Dalloz, 2014, p 47 (translation Geoffrey Samuel)

a) Formalism can refer to a mode of definition or to the delimitation of the object of analysis. *Stricto sensu*, a formalist delimitation of the object 'law' consists in analysing only the positive law and nothing but the positive law, in leaving aside social facts, history, natural law and moral principles. Such an approach is associated with different positivist currents. *Strictissimo sensu*, the formalist delimitation of the object reduces the analysis, within positive law, to the form and to the structures of legal systems and of norms. The study of the socio-political functions or contents of these norms is, then, left aside ...

One can see the immediate foundation of this legal formalism in the writings of the 17th- and 18th-century jurists such as Heineccius. However, these jurists belonged to what is called the school of natural law, which meant that they considered legal knowledge to be dualistic in its form. There were the positive laws of the region or country and there were higher laws which transcended these positive laws and which, like scientific laws, were part of nature. These two levels could sometimes conflict: an unjust law – that is a law that does not conform to the higher natural law – was said not to be law. This view was abandoned in the 19th century because such 'a dualism could not for a moment be admitted by any philosophy of law' (Jones, 1940, 205). This was because legal 'philosophy required unity and objectivity in its subject matter' and thus it 'must be consistently monistic'. For a 'rule either is or is not law; it cannot at the same time be both' (Jones, 1940, 206). Natural law theory was abandoned in favour of positivism; and along with this 'hardening' of formalism there was a further 'hardening' of reasoning method.

Véronique Champeil-Desplats, *Méthodologies du droit et des sciences du droit*, Dalloz, 2014, p 48 (translation Geoffrey Samuel)

f) Formalism can also refer to a certain representation of legal reasoning in general and judicial reasoning in particular. The latter takes the form of a syllogism. Inherited from Aristotelian logic, the syllogism, in its theory, consists in deducing from a general proposition (the major premise), under which is subsumed a particular proposition (the minor premise), a conclusion. If the two premise propositions are true, the conclusion is also true: 'All men are mortal' (major premise), Socrates is a man (minor premise), therefore Socrates is mortal (conclusion). On this model, judicial reasoning takes the form of what is said to be a practical syllogism, that is to say one that is geared towards an action. The major premise becomes, then, a general norm: 'all thieves must be punished', the minor premise is a particular proposition expressing a categorised fact ('Socrates is a thief'). From this is logically and mechanically deduced the conclusion: 'Socrates must be punished'.

This said, the 16th-century jurists equally realised, along with the Roman lawyers (see eg D.1.3, D.50.16), that words could be ambiguous. How should expressions be interpreted?

Digest of Justinian

Book 1 Title 3

17. CELSUS, *Digest, book 26.* To know statutes is not a matter of adhering to their words (*verba*), but of knowing their force and power (*vim ac potestatem*).

18. CELSUS, *Digest, book 29.* Benign interpretation should be given to statutes so as to conserve their intention (*voluntas*).

19. CELSUS, *Digest, book 33.* When a statute is ambiguous the meaning to be adopted is one which avoids undermining it, above all if the intention (*voluntas*) of the statute is able to be secured.

24. CELSUS, *Digest, book 9.* It is against the legal method to make a judgement or give an opinion on one particular part of a statute unless the whole statute has been taken into consideration.

29. PAUL, *Sole book on the Lex Cincia.* A person acts against a statute who does what the statute forbids; it is a fraud against the statute when one clings to the words (*verbis*) and evades the meaning (*sententiam*) of it. Furthermore nobody should be thought to have said what was not motivated by their mind (*non mente*) ...

Book 33 Title 10

7. CELSUS, *Digest, Book 19* ... 2 ... For my part I think nobody says what he does not intend (*non sentiret*), above all if a name be used which is applied to a sole object, for speech is used as our servant.

Book 50 Title 17

96. MAECIANUS, *Fideicommissa, Book 6.* In ambiguous speech, one must above all examine the intention (*sententia*) of the person who has spoken.

These Roman sources provide the starting point for interpretation of legal texts. What emerges from these sources is a tension between words (*verba*) and intention (*sententia* and *mens*); and this tension was to be taken up and developed by the later civilian jurists.

Donald Kelley, *The Human Measure: Social Thought in the Western Legal Tradition*, Harvard University Press, 1990, p 133 (endnotes omitted)

Put another way, this hermeneutical question concealed a[n] issue crucial to jurisprudence across the centuries, which was whether the construction of laws should be strict or liberal (*restrictiva* or *extensiva*). The consensus seems to be on the side of the 'more benign' as against 'rigorous' judgment. 'Interpretation should be not literal [*ad literam*]', wrote Baldus, 'but rather meaningful [*ad sensum*], for the sense of the words should prevail.' One should go beyond the literal *exposito vocabuli*, then, to the 'explanation of the true meaning [*ad verum intellectum*], understood according to the reason rather than the shell an exterior of the words.' The principle of judicial discretion also involved the complicated question of equity, which (according to an old rule) was the basis for interpreting laws and contracts (*fundamentum interpretandi leges et pacta*).

Thus three fundamental interpretative approaches grew out of the 16th-century writings of the civilian jurists. One could focus on the words of the text (*verba*); on the intention of the legislator (*mens legislatoris*); or on the rationality of the law as a whole in relation to the specific text (*ratio legis*) (inspired to some extent by D.1.3.24). We shall see that a fourth approach which was fashioned in more modern times was one that focused on the function of the statute, although this approach overlaps to some extent with the *mens legislatoris*.

Yet how could these interpretative ideas be reconciled with the *mos mathematicus* method which underpinned the syllogism?

Véronique Champeil-Desplats, *Méthodologies du droit et des sciences du droit*, Dalloz, 2014, pp 48–49 (translation Geoffrey Samuel)

g) Following on from this, formalism can also refer to a certain conception of interpretation of legal texts. 'Interpretative formalism' consists [in the words of S Castignone] in 'interpreting legal assertions' in a 'logico-systemic mode' in presupposing that one will be able to find in the meaning 'intrinsic in the norm (or system of norms) in question', 'the solution to a legal problem, in bypassing historical, teleological, economic, functional, and environmental factors or, in a word, any facts (which are considered to be) extrinsic'. ...

Thus with codification there was, at least at first, a certain fusing of the *mens legislatoris* with the *verba* of the code itself. The role of the jurist was no longer to search for general legal principles in the natural law, for they were now inherent in the texts of positive law. Interpretation and deduction became a 'scientific' exercise in that it was a matter of describing what was inherent in the legislative texts and applying these described norms and principles in a neutral (that is logical) fashion. In other words the hermeneutic (interpretation) dimension to legal reasoning became subservient to the logical process. 'The hermeneutical dimension', writes one jurist about 19th-century German legal thought, 'so essential to the legal science of the [German] historical school, is now only a secondary aspect, inferior and negligible to a true and pure scientific treatment of law' (Jouanjan, 2005, 229). Interpretation was considered, at least during the 19th century, as being too closely associated with factors now regarded extrinsic to law. This kind of attitude may be much less intense today in the civil law world, but it underpins the belief of those who think that the role of the judge can be computerised.

1.6 COMMON LAWYERS

In England things were different. The Roman texts had little or no influence in a procedural system where the main decisions, at least up to the 16th century, were taken by juries, for there was a jury in every common law case up until the end of the 19th century (see Samuel, 2014, 5–25). Where the common law was rather similar was in the way that its main focal point before the 19th century was the legal action. Nevertheless, these forms of action were very different to the Roman ones. Before the 18th century legal disputes tended to be about whether the right form of action had been brought.

Doige's Case (1442) YB Trin 20 Hen 6 6,f 34, pl 4 Exchequer Chamber
(translation CHS Fifoot)

Newton CJ: If I bail a certain sum of money to *Paston* to bail over to *Fortescue*, now, if *Paston*, does not do this, he will be liable to me in an action of Account and also in an action of Debt, and it is at my pleasure which I shall bring; but when I have brought the one, the other is extinguished. So in this case here there are two actions, Covenant and Deceit, and so the party may bring Deceit if he wishes …

Fortescue CJ: Willingly. I would agree that, if I buy a horse from you, now the property in the horse is in me, and for this you shall have a writ of Debt for the money and I shall have Detinue for the horse on this bargain. But that is not so in our case. For, though the plaintiff has a right to have his land in conscience, yet the land does not pass without livery. …

One might note how the problem of the sale and purchase of a horse is not being analysed in terms of a contract (contract of sale), as would be the case in a system governed by a law based on the Roman model. The case is analysed in terms of the remedies available to the seller of the horse (action in debt) and to the buyer (action in detinue). If a person made a promise which he later did not keep, this might give rise to an action for damages in covenant or deceit (later in a form of action known as assumpsit, an offshoot of trespass). This emphasis on the forms of action continued right up to the 19th century.

Michael Lobban, *The Common Law and English Jurisprudence 1760–1850*, Oxford University Press, 1991, p 9

At the beginning of the eighteenth century, most common lawyers did not seek to put their law into a rational form. Because they saw the law as a form of reasoning working within a set of remedies, most legal texts were written not in a systematic way, but as lists. The literature of the common law built from the bottom up, describing what law existed and assuming that it had an internal logic. The common law was seen to be based on the procedure of writs and actions as opposed to substantive laws or rights, so that the law was not seen as a self-contained whole, but developed in response to problems arising in society. Works outlining the various forms of writs were therefore a very important part of common law literature, ... Early eighteenth-century legal literature was dominated by the practitioners' books which displayed precedents of pleas. Such books did not attempt to describe legal rules for the practitioner – for 'rules' followed cases, not vice-versa – but neither did they attempt to analyse procedural rules. Instead, they merely showed the correct means with which to present a legal case, recording the pleas and the record of the averments in various cases without looking at all at the legal rules involved, the verdicts given, or the arguments of counsel. They were merely guides on how to draw up a good plea, for if the plea was correctly drawn, the case would be won ...

It was only during the 19th century that English lawyers started to see things in terms of contracts and torts. Indeed even as late as 1840 the law student learned the law by starting out from the *actio* (as the Romans called it).

Richard Garde, *Analysis of Pleading*, Maxwell, 1841, pp 1, 3–4

1. An action is the *legal* demand of a person's right. ...

4. Personal actions are those which are brought for the specific recovery of goods and chattels – or for damages, or other redress, for breach of contract, or other injuries of whatever description, except the recovery of lands, &c. ...

14. In personal actions, the most usual of which are assumpsit, debt, covenant, detinue, trespass, trespass on the case, trover, and replevin, the action in the inferior courts must be commenced by a writ of summons or a writ of capias …

17. *Action of debt* lies where a person claims the recovery of a *certain* sum of money alleged to be due to him, and is generally founded on some contract alleged to have taken place between the parties, or on some matter of fact from which the law implies a contract between them.

18. *Action of covenant* lies where a party claims damages for breach of *covenant*, ie of a promise under seal.

19. *Action of detinue* lies where a party claims the specific recovery of goods and chattels or deeds and writings detained from him.

20. *Action of assumpsit* lies where a party claims *damages* for a breach of simple contract, ie a promise not under seal. These promises may be expressed or implied, and the law always implies a promise to do that which a party is legally liable to perform.

21. *Action of trespass* lies where a party claims *damages* for a trespass, ie an injury committed with violence against him, and this violence may be either *actual* or *implied.*

22. *Action of trespass on the case* lies where a party sues for *damages* for any wrong or cause of complaint to which covenant or trespass will not apply.

23. *Action for trover* lies to recover goods and chattels, and in its form it claims damages for these goods and chattels found and converted to the defendant's own use …

It might be tempting to think that this form of reasoning founded on the *actio* has disappeared. However, care must be taken. We shall see that there is a remedies model of reasoning which is still very relevant (see 3.5). This said, in 1852 the forms of action were abolished (Common Law Procedure Act 1852 s 3) and this left the common law without its traditional structure. One might note also how Garde linked actions with the notion of a right.

Bryant v Herbert (1877) 3 CPD 389 Court of Appeal

Bramwell LJ: … [The Common Law Procedure Acts 1852–1860] did not abolish forms of action in words. The Common Law Commissioners recommended that: but it was supposed that, if adopted, the law would be shaken to its foundations; so that all that could be done was to provide as far as possible that, though forms of actions remained, there never should be a question what was the form. This was accomplished save as to this very question of costs in actions within the county court jurisdiction. Until the passing of the statute [County Courts Act] we are discussing, it was necessary to see if an action was *assumpsit*, case &c. But the Common Law Procedure Act having passed, and the forms of actions being practically abolished, the legislature pass this Act dropping the words '*assumpsit*, case', &c., and using the words 'founded on contract', 'founded on tort'. This shows to me that the substance of the matter was to be looked at. One may observe there is no middle term; the statute supposes all actions are founded either on contract or on tort. So that it is tort, if not contract, contract if not tort ...

As a result of the abolition of the forms of action the common lawyers looked to the civil law for inspiration. It is not that the judges regarded French or German law as directly applicable to England. They thought that the civil law provided a science of law that transcended particular national states; in other words the great concepts of law such as ownership, possession, contract and fault liability were as relevant to England as to any continental country. This thinking was equally encouraged by the appearance of textbooks on the law of contract during the 19th century. Today, therefore, the taxonomy of the law has changed, although some of the old forms of action have survived as 'causes of action'.

1.7 LEGAL REASONING IN THE COMMON LAW

As for legal reasoning itself, there were two sources. There were sources within the law and sources outside of it.

Michael Lobban, *The Common Law and English Jurisprudence 1760–1850*, Oxford University Press, 1991, pp 80–82

There were two types of legal argument used by the courts, often concurrently, in solving these cases. One was the form of argument internal to the law, where judges argued from precedents, analogies, and forms, in their desire to articulate the true 'law', and where they urged the need for stability and certainty in law. The second type was external to the law, for the courts held that, where a case had been sufficiently alleged, the courts could rule from the grounds of fitness and justice alone. It was not unusual for judges to make comments like '[c]ommon sense is sufficient to decide this case, without having recourse to any legal decisions on the subject'. For ultimately, the common law was a system of remedies, to correct any wrong, to adjudicate in the best manner for society and the litigants ...

There is a temptation to view the notion of precedent as being as old as the common law itself. This is misleading because up until the 16th century the most important decisions were taken, in the common law courts, by the jury, who did not give reasons for their verdicts. Judges, for their part, were really only concerned as to whether the right form of action had been chosen (see generally Baker, 2003).

Henderson v Merrett Syndicates Ltd [1995] 2 AC 145 House of Lords

Lord Goff: ... The situation in common law countries, including of course England, is exceptional, in that the common law grew up within a procedural framework uninfluenced by Roman law. The law was categorised by reference to the forms of action, and it was not until the abolition of the forms of action by the Common Law Procedure Act 1852 (15 & 16 Vict c 76) that it became necessary to reclassify the law in substantive terms. The result was that common lawyers did at last separate our law of obligations into contract and tort, though in so doing they relegated quasi-contractual claims to the status of an appendix to the law of contract, thereby postponing by a century or so the development of a law of restitution. Even then, there was no systematic reconsideration of the problem of concurrent claims in contract and tort. We can see the courts rather grappling with unpromising material drawn from the old cases in which liability in negligence derived largely from categories based upon the status of the defendant. In a sense, we must not be surprised; for no significant law faculties were established at our universities until the late 19th century, and so until then there was no academic opinion available to guide or stimulate the judges ...

So if one poses the question as to 'what legal reasoning has been' in the English courts, the answer is that, up until the 18th century, it was largely concerned with the boundaries of each form of action – or, more generally, if the right procedure had been followed. Furthermore, as there were no law faculties teaching the common law until the 19th century, there was no corps of professors writing books similar to those of the Roman or medieval jurists. Equally there were no systematisers until Sir William Blackstone (1723–1780), and his great *Commentaries* had little effect on practitioners.

J Gordley, Contract in Pre-commercial Societies and in Western History, _International Encyclopedia of Comparative Law_, Volume VII, Chapter 2
(footnotes omitted)

22. ... Another difference was that the Roman jurists addressed questions of substantive law without enmeshing them in questions of procedure. The English judges did not, in part because originally Common Law courts were not courts of general jurisdiction but heard only those cases brought before them by the King's writ. To receive a remedy the plaintiff had to fit his case within one of the forms of action on which he could bring a writ. Common Law became organised around writs rather than around types of obligations such as contract or tort.

Thus even in the late 18th century, English judges did not think in terms of a law of contract. They thought in terms of forms of action such as *assumpsit* and covenant.

Beginning in the late 18th century, this traditional structure changed dramatically. English law ceased to be the exclusive concern of judges and barristers. Beginning with *Blackstone*, it became a university subject ... The first treatise on contract law, written by *Powell* in 1790, was followed by a stream of others.

Moreover, the forms of action were abolished by statute. Supposedly, English judges still gave the plaintiff a remedy only when the traditional forms of action would have entitled him to receive one. But the treatise writers and eventually the judges came to think in terms of a law of contract rather than of covenant and *assumpsit*. They tried to give this law an intellectual coherence that it has previously lacked. They did so, in part, by trying to sharpen the statement of English law they found in the cases. They did so also by borrowing ideas from continental law books, either to clarify a traditional rule or to solve a problem that the Common Law judges had not addressed ... By the end of the 19th century ... the Common Law had acquired a new doctrinal structure largely by borrowing from the continent ...

The change from a system of forms of action to one of contract and tort engendered a new type of reasoning. Instead of reasoning about the form of a particular claim the judges started to reason applying what might be described as a theory of, say, negligence founded on the behaviour of the defendant.

Letang v Cooper [1965] 1 QB 232 Court of Appeal

Lord Denning MR: ... The truth is that the distinction between trespass and case is obsolete. We have a different sub-division altogether. Instead of dividing actions for personal injuries into trespass (direct damage) or case (consequential damage), we divide the causes of action now according as the defendant did the injury intentionally or unintentionally. If one man intentionally applies force directly to another, the plaintiff has a cause of action in assault and battery, or, if you so please to describe it, in trespass to the person. 'The least touching of another in anger is a battery,' per Holt CJ in *Cole v Turner*. If he does not inflict injury intentionally, but only unintentionally, the plaintiff has no cause of action today in trespass. His only cause of action is in negligence, and then only on proof of want of reasonable care. If the plaintiff cannot prove want of reasonable care, he may have no cause of action at all. Thus, it is not enough nowadays for the plaintiff to plead that 'the defendant shot the plaintiff.' He must also allege that he did it intentionally or negligently. If intentional, it is the tort of assault and battery. If negligent and causing damage, it is the tort of negligence.

This theory approach is particularly evident with respect to contract.

Foster v Wheeler (1887) 36 Ch D 695 Chancery Division

Kekewich J: … Definitions of 'contract' are to be found in the text-books, and I have consulted several of them, including an American one, that of Mr *Parsons*. They are all founded on, and many of them simply adopt, the definition given by *Pothier* in part I, ch 1, sec 1, of his work on Contracts. This is his definition, which I take from the English translation of Mr *WD Evans*: 'An agreement by which two parties reciprocally promise and engage, or one of them singly promises and engages to the other to give some particular thing, or to do or abstain from doing some particular act.' Mr *Pollock's* definition in his work on the same subject slightly differs from this, and is, in my opinion, more complete and more accurate. He defines a contract, or rather an agreement, to be 'an act in the law whereby two or more persons declare their consent as to any act or thing to be done or forborne by some or one of those persons for the use of the others or other of them;' and in commenting on this definition he explains what is intended by an act in the law, saying that it must be on the face of the matter capable of having legal effect and concerned with duties and rights which can be dealt with by a Court of Justice …

One might note the influence, first, of civil law writers (Pothier) and, secondly, of textbooks. Law is now being stated very much in terms of rules (*regulae iuris*). Legal reasoning becomes focused, inter alia, around the interpretation and application of a legal rule, often, since the 19th century, one set out in a statute.

Beswick v Beswick [1966] Ch 538 Court of Appeal
[1968] AC 58 House of Lords

Danckwerts LJ (Court of Appeal): … The definition of 'property' in s 205(1)(xx) 'includes any thing in action, and any interest in real or personal property'. The section replaces s 5 of the Real Property Act 1845 and applies to personal as well as real property. The Act of 1845 only applied to real property, and presumably there was some intelligible object in the extension. The new section obviously cannot be confined to covenants running with the land. Why should the section not be taken to mean what it says? There really is no ambiguity. The section says that 'A person may take … the benefit of … any agreement over or respecting land or other property, although he may not be named as a party to the conveyance or other instrument'. The section seems to have come as a shock to conventional lawyers who could not believe their eyes, but the section does say that a person not a party can take the benefit of a contract. Faced with the unexpected and unfamiliar there has been a tendency to take a timorous view of the provisions of this section …

Lord Guest (House of Lords): … It may be that the draftsman in incorporating the wide definition of 'property' into s 56 had overlooked the result which it would have on the effect of this section by extending it beyond its predecessor. I am constrained to hold that if s 56 is to replace the previous law in s 5 of the Act of

1845, this can only be done by limiting the word 'property' in s 56 to real property and thereby excluding the wide definition of 'property' contained in s 205(1)(xx). The result is that the respondent has, in my view, no right to sue on the agreement of 14th March 1962 in her individual capacity …

Michael Lobban, as we have seen, explained that traditionally there were two sources of reasoning used in the common law courts. One was internal to the law (precedents) and one external (natural justice, common sense, policy). Today reasoning about causes of action and rules could be said to be forms of reasoning internal to the law. Yet reasoning using sources external to the law is still to be found as we shall see (see 3.3). This said, the precedent system has since the 19th century become much more formalised.

***Council of Law Reporting v Att-Gen* [1972] Ch 73 Court of Appeal**

Buckley LJ: … What then does the evidence establish about the need for reliable law reports and the reasons for publishing them? As the uncontradicted evidence of Professor Goodhart makes clear, in a legal system such as ours, in which judges' decisions are governed by precedents, reported decisions are the means by which legal principles (other than those laid down by statutes) are developed, established and made known, and by which the application of those legal principles to particular kinds of facts are illustrated and explained. Reported decisions may be said to be the tissue of the body of our non-statutory law. Whoever, therefore, would carry out any anatomical researches upon our non-statutory corpus juris must do so by research amongst, and study of, reported cases.

Professor Goodhart recalls that Sir Frederick Pollock in his paper entitled *The Science of Case Law* published in 1882 pointed out that the study of law is a science in the same sense as physics or chemistry are sciences, and that the material with which it is concerned consists of individual cases which must be analysed and measured as carefully as is the material in the other sciences. At about the same time the 'case system' of teaching law was introduced at the Harvard Law School, which has since become generally adopted. Accurate and authoritative law reports are thus seen to be essential both for the advancement of legal education and the proper administration of justice. As Professor Goodhart says: 'Accuracy in The Law Reports is, therefore, as important for the science of law as is the accuracy of instruments in the physical sciences.'

The legal profession has from times long past been termed a learned profession, and rightly so, for no man can properly practise or apply the law who is not learned in that field of law with which he is concerned. He must have more than an aptitude and more than a skill. He must be learned in a sense importing true scholarship. In a system of law such as we have in this country this scholarship can only be acquired and maintained by a continual study of case law.

I agree with Foster J in thinking that, when counsel in court cites a case to a judge, counsel is not in any real sense 'educating' the judge, counsel performing the role of a teacher and the judge filling the role of a pupil; but I do not agree with him that the process should not be regarded as falling under the charitable head of 'the advancement of education.' ...

This 'science' would appear to be one founded on case law. But care must be taken today. The 'case system' at Harvard is, since the American Realists (see 4.1), probably no longer seen as a 'science' akin to the natural sciences; and a question can now be raised as to whether cases, as opposed to statutes, are the primary source of English law.

1.8 INTERPRETATION OF STATUTES

The common law has of course traditionally been regarded as being based upon cases and precedents. Before the 19th century this was largely true, but today the position is dramatically different. By far the most important source of law in England is legislation and the great majority of cases decided by the courts involve the interpretation and application of a legislative text. Statutory interpretation is thus central to judging and reasoning in the English courts. However the courts, historically, have the power only to interpret; the judges do not have the constitutional power – as some continental constitutional courts have – to strike down legislation on the grounds that it violates the constitution.

***In re K (A Child)* [2001] 2 WLR 1141 Court of Appeal**

Judge LJ: ... **119** During the course of the argument I described the submission as 'stunning'. The time we have taken to reflect on our judgments has not diminished my sense of astonishment. In fairness to Miss de Haas I must briefly explain why.

120 If the argument were correct the implementation of the Human Rights Act 1998, on 2 October 2000, would have produced a constitutional earthquake. Parliament would have undermined the principle of parliamentary sovereignty, and revived Sir Edward Coke CJ's dictum in *Bonham's Case* (1610) 8 Co Rep 114a, 118a that 'the common law will control Acts of Parliament and sometimes adjudge them to be utterly void', a principle identified by Coke in order to impose some fetter on the extravagant royal concept of the prerogative, a controversy eventually settled in this country by the Revolution of 1688. And it would effectively 'set the judicial power above that of the legislature', emphatically described in 1765 by Blackstone in the 1st edition of his *Commentaries*, some 150 years before universal adult suffrage was established, as 'subversive of all government': BL Com, 1st ed, p 91 (For a still vivid analysis of *Bonham's Case* in its historical context, the relationship of the legislature and the judiciary, and the development of divergent constitutional routes in this country and the United States of America, see T F T Plucknett's article, first published in (1926) 40 Harv L Rev 30, 'Bonham's Case and Judicial Review', in *Studies in English Legal History* (1983), ch 14.)

121 It may on another occasion be appropriate to examine whether the sovereignty of Parliament empowers it to dispense with or divest itself of its own or any part of its sovereignty, but so far as the Human Rights Act 1998 is concerned, this question simply does not arise. Neither this nor any other court is empowered to repeal or amend, ignore or act contrary to any single statute, or any part of any statute. To the contrary: the Act is carefully drafted to ensure that the court cannot and must not strike down or dispense with any single item of primary legislation.

The rule is that Parliament is supreme and the judges have to apply a statutory provision. Nevertheless they have reserved the power to interpret such provisions. What methods do they employ when doing this?

R (Quintavalle) v Secretary of State for Health **[2003] 2 AC 687**
House of Lords

Lord Bingham: … **8.** The basic task of the court is to ascertain and give effect to the true meaning of what Parliament has said in the enactment to be construed. But that is not to say that attention should be confined and a literal interpretation given to the particular provisions which give rise to difficulty. Such an approach not only encourages immense prolixity in drafting, since the draftsman will feel obliged to provide expressly for every contingency which may possibly arise. It may also (under the banner of loyalty to the will of Parliament) lead to the frustration of that will, because undue concentration on the minutiae of the enactment may lead the court to neglect the purpose which Parliament intended to achieve when it enacted the statute. Every statute other than a pure consolidating statute is, after all, enacted to make some change, or address some problem, or remove some blemish, or effect some improvement in the national life. The court's task, within the permissible bounds of interpretation, is to give effect to Parliament's purpose. So the controversial provisions should be read in the context of the statute as a whole, and the statute as a whole should be read in the historical context of the situation which led to its enactment.

Lord Steyn: … **21.** … The pendulum has swung towards purposive methods of construction. This change was not initiated by the teleological approach of European Community jurisprudence, and the influence of European legal culture generally, but it has been accelerated by European ideas: see, however, a classic early statement of the purposive approach by Lord Blackburn in *River Wear Commissioners v Adamson* (1877) 2 App Cas 743, 763. In any event, nowadays the shift towards purposive interpretation is not in doubt. The qualification is that the degree of liberality permitted is influenced by the context, eg social welfare legislation and tax statutes may have to be approached somewhat differently …

> **Lord Millett:** ... **38.** The question is one of statutory construction. In construing a statute the task of the court is to ascertain the intention of Parliament as expressed in the words it has chosen. The Parliamentary intention is to be derived from the terms of the Act as a whole read in its context. Once it has been ascertained, the court must give effect to it so far as the legislative text permits.
>
> **39.** The search in every case is for what Parliament did intend, not what it would have intended had it foreseen later developments. ...

Two traditional focal points emerge from the common law's view of statutory interpretation: there is the emphasis on the intention of Parliament (*mens legislatoris*), but this intention is to be gathered primarily from the words used in the statute itself (*verba*). In other words common lawyers have merged *mens legislatoris* with the *verba.* This said, Lord Steyn seems to be suggesting a move towards a functional or purposive approach. Nevertheless it would probably be a mistake to think that a literal approach (*verba*) has been displaced, as we shall see (see 2.4).

1.9 LEGACY OF THE PAST

So what has legal reasoning been? Several models can be induced out of the historical material presented in this chapter. These models will be looked at in more detail in the chapters that follow but they may be summarised as follows:

- **Remedies** (*actio*). Early Roman and common law reasoning was centred on the legal action or, to use today's term, remedy. One can talk of a remedies model. In such a model the remedy is seen as the key institution in that it largely forms the subject matter of legal taxonomy (true of both early Roman and common law) and it acts as the starting point for the analysis of litigation facts.
- **Rules** (*regulae iuris*). The last title of the *Digest* is headed *de regulis iuris*, that is to say it concerns general rules of law (maxims). The *Institutes* of Justinian also set out the law in terms of general propositions. By the 16th century these *regulae iuris* had been elevated from mere summaries of the law (the Roman view: D.50.17.1) to a source of law in turn giving rise to the rule model of reasoning. (See further 2.1.)
- **Interpretation** (*interpretatio*). An early title (D.1.3) and the penultimate title to the *Digest* (D.50.16) are devoted (in whole or in part) to the method of interpretation and to the meaning of words.

There are other extracts also dealing with interpretation. The 16th-century civil lawyers spent much time and energy on the issues surrounding interpretation with the result that this notion of *interpretatio* became a focal point for reasoning techniques.

- **Rights** (*ius*). Later civil lawyers abandoned actions and started to explain law from the position of substantive law (*ius*) as viewed from the individual – that is to say from the viewpoint of what is ours and what is owed to us. This rights model became another focal point of legal reasoning and was particularly powerful in 20th-century legal thought.
- **Policy** (*utilitas*). The Romans never really developed any idea of policy reasoning in the modern sense of the expression, but they did justify some legal propositions on the basis of their utility rather than their strict rationality. It was the common law judges who were prepared to adopt a functionalist approach to decision making and this policy model remains of considerable importance in contemporary common law reasoning.
- **Interest** (*interesse*). Another Roman notion that subsequently became a focal point for reasoning was an interest. This expression was used by Roman jurists as a means of determining damage and loss in compensation claims, but in later legal thought it acquired an independence of its own. It became particularly valuable with the development of economics as a discipline since this subject is founded on the notion of interest. Interest provides, then, a valuable bridge between law and economics; yet it is equally an important notion in itself as a descriptive reasoning device.

These focal points – all of which can be traced back to Roman law via the later civilians – do not of course fully explain the complexities of legal reasoning. Far from it. They are simply starting points for thinking about judging; they are what might be called framework models. Reasoning techniques such as induction, deduction and analogy must equally be examined, as must more theoretical orientations such as schemes of intelligibility and paradigm orientations.

FURTHER READING AND QUESTIONS

1. An excellent overview of the history of civilian legal thought is to be found in Jones (1940) and in Stein (1999). See also Johnston (2015). A more detailed analysis of the reasoning of the civilian jurists is to be found in Gordley (2013). On the 19th century see

Stein (1980). As for the history of the common law, see Milsom (1981) and Baker (2002). On the 18th and 19th centuries see Lobban (1991). A short introduction to the common law is to be found in Samuel (2013).

2. Did the medieval Roman lawyers (the Glossators and Post-glossators or Commentators) reason in an identical way as the Roman jurists or were their methods rather different? (See Berman, 1983, and Gordley, 2013.)
3. Have there been 'revolutions' in the history of legal thought and reasoning? (Cf Maclean, 1992.)
4. When did jurists start to reason in terms of legal rights? (See Jolowicz, 1957, 61–81.)
5. 'It would seem, in fact, that in the seventeenth century, which was a great judicial era, theories of legal classification took very much the place of those theories of law reform which so occupied the minds of the last generation of Englishmen. The continuous activity of legislatures is an altogether modern phenomenon; ... The improvement in view was thus rather a reform of law-books than a reform of law' (Maine, 1890, 362–363). Is this an accurate view of the civil law?
6. Why is it that reasoning in the common law tradition does not seem to have been affected by 16th-century humanist writers? (Cf Baker, 2003.)
7. Did legal reasoning in the common law profoundly change in the 16th century? Did it change in the 19th century? (See Baker, 2003; Lobban, 1991; Ibbetson, 1999.)

2. Judging and legal reasoning today ('official portrait') (1)

Roman law might not be directly relevant to the common law but it was the basis of European 'legal science'. This science was to be very influential on common law thought during the 19th century which saw the abolition of the forms of action. Thus Roman legal thinking, as developed by the medieval and later jurists, helped shape what might be called the models of legal reasoning. Various models, as we have seen (see 1.9), can be traced back to the Roman lawyers as interpreted by the later European jurists.

2.1 RULE MODEL

The *Digest* of Roman law largely consists of practical cases. The Romans developed a whole range of legal concepts such as ownership, possession, contract and so on but rather than define them they preferred to test them with reference to factual examples. Nevertheless the very last title to the *Digest* is called *De regulis iuris*, which means 'rules of law'. Thus if one asks what it is to have legal knowledge, the answer that one might often receive – although not from the Romans themselves (see D.50.17.1) – is this. Law is a matter of rules; and thus learning the law is learning and applying legal rules. There are plenty of legal theorists who subscribe to and support this vision of legal knowledge.

R Susskind, *Expert Systems in Law*, Oxford University Press, 1987, pp 78–79, 173

Before proceeding, however, one fundamental assumption ... should be articulated: that *rules* do and should play a central role in legal science, legal knowledge representation, and in legal reasoning. Overwhelming authority for this proposition can be found in legal theory, and even a philosopher such as Dworkin, who has questioned the sufficiency of rules for legal decision-making, does nevertheless himself seem to presuppose a predominant place for them, as MacCormick has shown. If this is so, and rules have, as MacCormick alleges, 'logical primacy', then surely it should be sought, in the first instance, to represent legal knowledge in rule form ...

... All legal theorists, it is submitted, operate within a rule-based paradigm: they share the background assumption that clear cases can be solved through the application of rules ...

The primary function of a judge is, accordingly, to find and to apply the appropriate rules to the relevant facts of a litigation dispute.

***Derby & Co v Weldon (No 5)* [1989] 1 WLR 1244 Chancery Division**

Vinelott J: ... The function of a judge of first instance is to find the relevant facts and, with the assistance of counsel, to ascertain the law as set out in any relevant statutory provisions and in principles to be derived from the decisions of the House of Lords and the Court of Appeal, and to draw the appropriate legal consequences. It is not open to the judge in performing this primary function to consider, far less express an opinion, as to the correctness of a decision of the Court of Appeal or the House of Lords except in those rare cases where he is faced with conflicting decisions of the Court of Appeal and must choose which to follow. That does not rest solely upon the feelings of deference and respect with which a judge of first instance will naturally and properly approach a decision of the Court of Appeal or the House of Lords. An opinion which the judge may entertain as to the correctness or otherwise of, for instance, the interpretation of a decision of the House of Lords by the Court of Appeal, is simply irrelevant to his primary duty which is to ascertain the statutory provisions and the principles stated in decisions that are binding on him which govern the case before him ...

Having discovered both the relevant facts and the appropriate rule or rules, the next step is to apply the rule to the facts.

2.2 APPLYING THE RULE MODEL

This application process is traditionally – according to the formalist model of law – regarded as a matter of syllogistic logic (see 1.5). In describing this formalism one was looking, it may be recalled, at the civil (continental) legal tradition. But this syllogistic analysis finds expression in the common law world as well.

***Lupton v FA & AB Ltd* [1972] AC 634 House of Lords**

Lord Simon: ... A judicial decision will often be reached by a process of reasoning which can be reduced into a sort of complex syllogism, with the major premise consisting of a pre-existing rule of law (either statutory or judge-made) and with the minor premise consisting of the material facts of the case under immediate consideration. The conclusion is the decision of the case, which may or may not establish new law – in the vast majority of cases it will be merely the application of existing law to the facts judicially ascertained. Where the decision does constitute new law, this may or may not be expressly stated as a proposition of law: frequently the new law will appear only from subsequent comparison of, on the one hand, the material facts inherent in the major premise with, on the other, the material facts which constitute the minor premise. As a result of this comparison it will often be apparent that a rule has been extended by an analogy expressed or implied. I take as an example … *National Telephone Co v Baker* [1893] 2 Ch 186. Major premise: the rule in *Rylands v Fletcher* (1866) LR 1 Exch 265, (1868) LR 3 HL 330. Minor premise: the defendant brought and stored electricity on his land for his own purpose; it escaped from the land; in so doing it injured the plaintiff's property. Conclusion: the defendant is liable in damages to the plaintiff (or would have been but for statutory protection). Analysis shows that the conclusion establishes a rule of law, which may be stated as 'for the purpose of the rule in *Rylands v Fletcher* electricity is analogous to water' or 'electricity is within the rule in *Rylands v Fletcher*'. That conclusion is now available as the major premise in the next case, in which some substance may be in question which in this context is not perhaps clearly analogous to water but is clearly analogous to electricity. In this way, legal luminaries are constituted which guide the wayfarer across uncharted ways.

In order for syllogistic logic to operate unambiguously what is required is a closed system of 'axioms'.

Kevin Gray and Susan Gray, The Rhetoric of Reality, in J Getzler (ed), *Rationalizing Property, Equity and Trusts*, Butterworths, 2003, pp 204, 208–209 (footnotes omitted)

There is much to be said for the view that … law comprises an axiomatic system of rules in which legal outcomes emerge as the sweet distillation of an invincible logical process. As Lord Devlin once pointed out, 'no system of law can be workable if it has not got logic at the root of it'. Logic, with all its frailty, is still the essential operating system of the human condition – our ultimate operational resource. Logic is commonly seen as providing a universal standard by which it can be judged whether a particular conclusion has been correctly derived from its supposed premises. Indeed, the very universality of the logical process goes far towards ensuring both our freedom from the exercise of arbitrary will and a measure of equality in the enforcement of the law – in short, towards guaranteeing that we have a government of laws and not of men … Logical systems tend, furthermore, to satisfy that component of the 'moral emotion of justice' which causes humans to desire that 'the proposition by which conduct is evaluated be taken as the consequence of some larger, more general, proposition' (Max Radin) …

The essence of an axiomatic structure is, of course, that 'axioms' (or 'fixed postulates') enjoy a fundamental and autonomous status within the scheme. An axiomatic proposition is a raw *datum* whose validity is assumed, never proved.

> One can no more seek to go *behind* an axiom than one may question why, in a game of chess, the knight or the bishop moves in the peculiar ways these pieces do. It is irrelevant that the axiom in question is morally neutral or indifferent and that no evil of any kind would ensue from a denial of its validity. Axioms are simply immune from rational challenge. To knock at an axiom is to want to play a different game; and to alter an axiom is already to have begun a different game ...

This need for an axiomatic structure is the reason why many jurists, both in the past and today, search for a coherence and system in legal rules. In this 'axiomatic' rule model of judging, the judge is seen as neutral; he or she is simply applying a rule through the use of logic. Political and (or) social bias are thus excluded.

2.3 INTERPRETATION MODEL

The idea that legal rules are like mathematical axioms largely fell out of favour in the 20th century. Linguistic propositions could never have the certainty of numbers since language can often be ambiguous. A notice declaring 'No vehicles in the Park' gives rise to questions on the meaning of 'vehicle' and 'in'. A small child enters on his little tricycle: has the rule been infringed? An ambulance enters the park in order to provide emergency assistance to a heart-attack victim: has the rule been infringed? The front wheel of someone's motorcycle crosses the boundary line into the park: has the rule been infringed? These ambiguities created by linguistic propositions (rules) provoked a shift of focus within the rule model of law. Judging was seen less as a matter of logic and more as a question of interpretation. This is particularly true, of course, where the law is contained in a written text such as a statute, a will or a contract; but precedent, equally, became a matter of interpretation.

> **Ronald Dworkin, *A Matter of Principle*, Oxford University Press, 1985, p 146**
>
> I shall argue that legal practice is an exercise in interpretation not only when lawyers interpret particular documents or statutes but generally. Law so conceived is deeply and thoroughly political. Lawyers and judges cannot avoid politics in the broad sense of political theory. But law is not a matter of personal and partisan politics, and a critique of law that does not understand this difference will provide poor understanding and even poorer guidance. I propose that we can improve our understanding of law by comparing legal interpretation with interpretation in other fields of knowledge, particularly literature. I also

expect that law, when better understood, will provide a better grasp of what interpretation is in general.

Ronald Dworkin (1931–2013) was perhaps one of the most famous contemporary theorists who regarded legal reasoning entirely as an interpretative process. This is not to assert that this was the only model he advocated; he also argued that judges should concern themselves only with the rights of the parties, these rights being identified as a matter of interpretation.

2.4 INTERPRETING TEXTS

The interpretation model is central when it comes to applying written legal provisions such as statutes, contracts and wills. Statutory interpretation is a subject area in itself (see 1.8) and, as we have seen, the emphasis is primarily on the words of the text.

Murray v Foyle Meats Ltd **[1999] 3 WLR 356 House of Lords (N Ireland)**

Lord Clyde: My Lords, it is an elementary rule in the interpretation and the application of statutory provisions that it is to the words of the legislation that attention must primarily be directed. Generally it will be the ordinary meaning of the words which will require to be adopted. On appropriate occasions it may be proper as matter of interpretation to adopt extended meanings to words or phrases, particularly if thereby the purpose of the legislation can be best effected or the validity of the legislation preserved. On other occasions it may be appropriate to adopt a strict or narrow meaning of the language used. But whatever the intensity of the process the temptation of substituting other expressions for the words of the statute in the course of interpreting it is to be discouraged, however attractive such a course may seem to be by way of explaining what it is thought the legislature is endeavouring to say. It may certainly be useful to analyse a statutory provision so as to identify the successive elements of which it is composed and so focus attention on the particular word or words which call for interpretation, or isolate the particular requirements which have to be met for its application ... But such an exercise should not involve any significant departure from the actual language which has been used.

When it comes to a matter of applying a statutory provision to particular circumstances it may be tempting to devise so-called tests for its application. In the context of the particular area of employment law with which the present appeal is concerned the labels of a 'contract test' and a 'function test' have been identified. But the only test for the application of a statutory provision, such as occurs in the present case, is whether or not on a proper construction of the statutory language the facts which have been established fall within the provision. I see no advantage in prescribing labels as a means of giving

> guidance to the method to be adopted in applying the provision. Once the statute has been properly construed its application does not depend upon any test but on the language used and the particular facts and circumstances of the case. On the other hand there is in my view a danger in prescribing and designating tests since they may encourage an approach not intended by the legislator …

As we shall see, this is a very good example of a 'text-activated' theory (see 6.6). It is all very well to say that one must focus on the words of the legal text, but, as we have seen, this does not solve all the problems of meaning (see 1.8). The interpretation and meaning model is more complex. Continental learning, as we have seen (see 1.5), identified three possible approaches; and at a very general level what seems to emerge from the medieval and Enlightenment jurists is a series of dialectical oppositions between the words of a text (*verba*), the spirit of the law (*ratio iuris*) and the intention of the legislator (*mens legislatoris*). A more modern opposition is the one between the literal word and the purpose or *function* of the text, although this may well overlap with the intention of the author of the text. In short, does one look at: (1) the dictionary meaning of the word; (2) the intention of the legislator (or contractor or testator); (3) the apparent purpose of the statute; or (4) the word within its more general textual or legal context? When two judges differ over the meaning of a word or phrase, it is usually because one judge may be applying, say, approach (1) above while the other judge is employing, for example, approach (3). One might add a further approach: what does the 'reasonable reader' think?

> ***R v East Sussex County Council* [2015] UKSC 7 Supreme Court**
>
> **Lord Neuberger and Lord Hodge**: … 58. A prohibition can be expressed in such a way as to imply a permission. For instance, it is hard to argue against the proposition that a byelaw which states that dogs must be kept on a lead in a public park implies a permission to bring dogs into the park, provided that they are kept on a lead. It is at least as a matter of pure linguistic logic, possible to interpret the byelaw as solely meaning that, if (and only if) specific permission is obtained from the park authority by a person to bring a dog into the park, then the byelaw will apply. However, any reasonable reader of the byelaw would not consider that it had such a limited meaning. In other words, as with any question of interpretation, a strictly logical linguistic analysis of the words concerned cannot prevail over a contextual assessment of what they would naturally convey to an ordinary and reasonable speaker of English.

The role of the reader can be as important as the role of the author when it comes to interpretation of a text. Indeed this has given rise, in film studies, to a theory known as reception theory (see 6.6). However there are occasions when judges, for constitutional reasons, might adopt a narrow approach, even though the words of the text itself do not necessarily force one into such a narrow interpretation.

Birmingham CC v Oakley [2001] 1 AC 617 House of Lords

Lord Hoffmann: My Lords, on the surface, this does not look like a very momentous case. The question is whether Mr and Mrs Oakley's landlord should have provided them with a basin in the WC. The statute which they say made it necessary to install one is ambiguous. The language is capable of bearing such a construction. On the other hand, it is very unlikely that this was what Parliament intended. So the courts have a choice. If they say that Mr and Mrs Oakley should have had a basin, landlords of old houses and flats all over the country will have to install them. Local authorities and housing trusts will have to incur very considerable expense. Under the surface, therefore, the case raises a question of great constitutional importance. When it comes to the expenditure of large sums of public and private money, who should make the decision? If the statute is clear, then of course Parliament has already made the decision and the courts merely enforce it. But when the statute is doubtful, should judges decide? Or should they leave the decision to democratically elected councillors or members of Parliament? ...

Lord Steyn (dissenting): ... The distinction between layout and state of the premises is not to be found in the statute, and it is certainly not indicated by the language of the provision or the context. It is on analysis no more than a verbal technique to cut down the generality of the wording of the modern statute. The justices were entitled to find that the premises were themselves inadequate so far as health and hygiene were concerned. Acknowledging that it is not an easy question, I prefer the broader approach of Lord Clyde to the narrow view of the majority. For the reasons Lord Clyde gives I would dismiss the appeal.

Lord Millett: My Lords, I have had the advantage of reading in draft the speeches of my noble and learned friends Lord Slynn of Hadley and Lord Hoffmann, with which I am in full agreement. In my view the Public Health Acts are concerned with the state of the premises, not with their layout or with the facilities which ought to be installed in them. In the present case the risk to health can be variously ascribed to the layout of the premises (because the lavatory was poorly sited) or to the absence of a desirable facility (a washbasin in reasonable proximity to the lavatory). But it does not derive from the state of the premises ...

Two important aspects of legal reasoning are in evidence in the above case. First, there is the delicate constitutional position of judges; the interpretation of law often amounts to making or extending law. This is delicate, as Lord Hoffmann points out, because judges are unelected. Human rights law presents particular problems in this respect, although of course it was politicians who voted into law the Human Rights Act 1998. Secondly, there is the use of the dialectical method; the majority define 'state' of the premises not by looking at a dictionary but by setting up a contrasting word, namely 'layout'. Once a dichotomy between state and layout is established it permits the interpreter to escape from having to apply the statutory text to the facts (but see Lord Steyn). However, as we have seen, the judges normally prefer a contextual approach to a literal one. Yet this contextual approach can sometimes come into conflict with a literal approach. Is two inches of water covering a bathroom or kitchen floor a 'flood'? The occupier, on discovering the water, is likely to declare that the 'room is flooded'.

***Young v Sun Alliance and London Insurance Ltd* [1977] 1 WLR 104**
Court of Appeal

Shaw LJ: ... The plaintiff appeals to this court on the ground that the judge erred in his construction of the word 'flood' in the context in which it appeared in the policy. Mr Jacob has put before this court a most able argument, and an almost persuasive one, to the effect that in this context, notwithstanding the juxtaposition of those three words, 'storm, tempest or flood.' which appear to denote different forms of violent manifestation of some natural phenomenon, 'flood' here, when one is considering its application in relation to a private dwelling, ought to be construed in a wide rather than a narrow sense. First because the language was adopted by the insurers so that the contra proferentem principle should apply, and secondly because, so far as a householder is concerned, if he finds that in part of his property he cannot walk about except by putting his feet into 3 inches of water, and if that happens in a significant part of his property, then he is entitled to say that it has been flooded; and if any damage results from it, the damage has resulted from or has been caused by flood.

At first sight – or perhaps I should say at second sight having heard Mr Jacob's argument – that appears to be a plausible proposition. But on further consideration it seems apparent that what the policy was intending to cover, whatever may be the colloquial use of the word 'flood' in common parlance, were three forms of natural phenomena which were related not only by the fact that they were natural, but also that they were unusual manifestations, certainly of those phenomena: that is to say, 'storm' meant 'rain accompanied by strong wind'; 'tempest' denoted an even more violent storm; and 'flood' was not something which came about by seepage or by trickling or dripping from some natural source, but involved 'an overflowing or irruption of a great body of water' as one of the definitions in the Shorter Oxford English Dictionary, 3rd ed. (1944), puts it. The slow movement of water, which can often be detected so that the loss threatened can be limited, is very different from the sudden onset of water where nothing effective can be done to prevent the loss, for it happens too quickly.

It is because the word 'flood' occurs in the context it does, that I have come to the conclusion that one must go back to first impressions, namely, that it is used there in the limited rather than the wider sense; that it means something which is a natural phenomenon which has some element of violence, suddenness or largeness about it.

If that is the right view, it disposes of the matter. It is the view which was taken by the judge, who expressed very much the same idea about the meaning of the word 'flood' in this connection. I see no reason, after reflection, to differ from the judge, and accordingly I would dismiss the appeal.

Lawton LJ: This appeal raises a semantic problem which has troubled many philosophers for centuries, and it can, I think, be expressed in the aphorism that an elephant is difficult to define but easy to recognise. I find difficulty in defining the word 'flood' as used in this policy; I have no difficulty in looking at the evidence in this case and coming to the conclusion, as I do, that the water in the lavatory was not a flood within the meaning of paragraph 8 of this policy.

Mr Day pointed out to the court that the phrase in the policy is 'Storm, tempest or flood,' and that the word 'flood' is used as a word in ordinary English usage to cover a situation which may be very different from the situations to which the words 'flooded' or 'flooding' are appropriate. I agree. It is not without relevance that paragraph 9, the next paragraph in the policy, refers to the 'Escape of water from or frost damage to any water, drainage or heating installation.' So 'flood' is something different for the purposes of this policy from an 'escape of water.'

I agree with Shaw LJ that the essence of 'flood' in ordinary English is some abnormal, violent situation. It may not necessarily have to be sudden, but it does, in my judgment, have to be violent and abnormal. This seepage of water through a rise in the water level was not violent, and it was not all that abnormal; it was the sort of incident which householders sometimes have to suffer as a result of 'rising damp.'

I, too, would dismiss the appeal.

Cairns LJ: I also would dismiss the appeal. It is not necessary to decide in this case whether the interpretation of the word 'flood' in an insurance policy is a matter of law, or whether the problem is to be approached in the way that Lord Reid in *Cozens v Brutus* [1973] AC 854, 861 approached the meaning of the word 'insulting,' because there is apparently no previous decision of the court as to the meaning of the word 'flood' in this context. Therefore, the only way in which one can interpret it is by asking oneself what is the meaning that an ordinary Englishman reading this word in the context in which it appears would give to it. I think in such circumstances one's first impression may be the best guide to the real meaning. Giving oneself for the moment the credit of assuming that one is an ordinary Englishman, when I first looked at this case my reaction to it was: 'No; you really could not call this a flood.' But when one began to analyse it, and to listen to the argument of Mr Jacob, I, like Shaw LJ, was almost persuaded that this could be called a flood. That it could be called a flooded floor, that an ordinary man or an ordinary housewife would say, 'The water is flooding my floor,' I have no doubt. But we come back to the question: Is it a flood? Is it a flood in a clause which refers also to 'storm and tempest'? – which I think, contributes to giving a colour to the meaning of it.

I think it is very largely a question of degree. Mr Day made it the main part of his concise argument before us that a flood involved a large quantity of water. That seems to me to be right. I do not think that water 3 inches deep in a room 6 ft. by 4 ft. would be regarded by any normal person in the context of this policy as a flood. Therefore, I agree with Shaw and Lawton LJJ that the appeal fails.

The text in issue in this case was not a statute but a contract. However, similar interpretation problems arise in written contracts as in statutes. Does one focus on the words in the contract (*verba*) or does one try to seek out the contracting parties' intentions (*voluntas*)? In Roman law much depended upon whether the words were in themselves clear or whether they were ambiguous (D.32.25.1). Nevertheless the basic rule in civil law is that one does not stop at the words; one seeks out the intention of the parties (D.50.16.219; CC art 1188) summed up in the expression *id quod actum est* (roughly: what was actually agreed) (see Zimmermann, 1996, 621–642). It is, however, not just a question of textual interpretation; there is also a factual question. What constitutes, as a fact, a 'flood'? Is this a question of interpretation or is it one of definition? Can one distinguish between the two? One is back at meaning. What did the parties mean by the word 'flood'?

***Chartbrook Ltd v Persimmon Homes Ltd* [2009] 1 AC 1101**
House of Lords

Lord Hoffmann: ... **14** There is no dispute that the principles on which a contract (or any other instrument or utterance) should be interpreted are those summarised by the House of Lords in *Investors Compensation Scheme Ltd v West Bromwich Building Society* [1998] 1 WLR 896, 912–913. They are well known and need not be repeated. It is agreed that the question is what a reasonable person having all the background knowledge which would have been available to the parties would have understood them to be using the language in the contract to mean. The House emphasised that 'we do not easily accept that people have made linguistic mistakes, particularly in formal documents' (similar statements will be found in *Bank of Credit and Commerce International SA v Ali* [2002] 1 AC 251, 269; *Kirin-Amgen Inc v Hoechst Marion Roussel Ltd* [2005] 1 All ER 667, 681–682 and *Jumbo King Ltd v Faithful Properties Ltd* (1999) 2 HKCFAR 279, 296) but said that in some cases the context and background drove a court to the conclusion that 'something must have gone wrong with the language'. In such a case, the law did not require a court to attribute to the parties an intention which a reasonable person would not have understood them to have had.

There are occasions when the language used in the contract seems to have 'gone wrong'. But such a consideration must be weighed against the professional context in which business contracting takes place. With a statute, especially one that results from a compromise within a divided legislature, the unelected judges have to be wary about reopening debates that were themselves controversial. The legislature has spoken and the courts can only focus upon the text that finally emerges. A similar issue can arise in the commercial domain.

The Chikuma [1981] 1 WLR 314 House of Lords

Lord Bridge: ... It has often been pointed out that shipowners and charterers bargain at arm's length. Neither class has such a preponderance of bargaining power as to be in a position to oppress the other. They should be in a position to look after themselves by contracting only on terms which are acceptable to them. Where, as here, they embody in their contracts common form clauses, it is, to my mind, of overriding importance that their meaning and legal effect should be certain and well understood. The ideal at which the courts should aim, in construing such clauses, is to produce a result, such that in any given situation both parties seeking legal advice as to their rights and obligations can expect the same clear and confident answer from their advisers and neither will be tempted to embark on long and expensive litigation in the belief that victory depends on winning the sympathy of the court. This ideal may never be fully attainable, but we shall certainly never even approximate to it unless we strive to follow clear and consistent principles and steadfastly refuse to be blown off course by the supposed merits of individual cases.

A literal approach (*verba*) cannot therefore be dismissed as outdated since the context in which written legal texts are formulated can sometimes be of overriding importance. Such an approach might itself be seen as a form of justice.

Fothergill v Monarch Airlines Ltd [1981] AC 251 House of Lords

Lord Diplock: ... Elementary justice or ... the need for legal certainty demands that the rules by which a citizen is to be bound should be ascertainable by him (or, more realistically, by a competent lawyer advising him) ...

In these last two extracts it should be noted how the judges refer to lawyers advising clients. Clients should be able to obtain clear advice as to their rights and obligations. Yet does this mean that the law is being declared not just by judges but also by firms and chambers of lawyers? Should one see interpretation as being an exercise that takes place within an 'interpretative community'? In other words does the community have expectations with regard to the judges while the judges have expectations with regard to the legal profession and, through them, their clients? However, this raises a further question. Should different kinds of statutes (or indeed different types of contract) elicit different types of interpretation? For example, might constitutional statutes be subject to different rules of interpretation than, say, commercial law regulatory texts? Human rights certainly have created a special interpretative rule.

Human Rights Act 1998

3. Interpretation of legislation

(1) So far as it is possible to do so, primary legislation and subordinate legislation must be read and given effect in a way which is compatible with the Convention rights.

This statutory provision indicates that the process of interpretation can itself be the subject of rules.

2.5 RULES OF INTERPRETATION

From what has been said so far judges would appear to have some methodological leeway when it comes to interpretation. However can such leeway be controlled by the law itself? Are there 'rules' about how to interpret?

***R v Secretary of State for the Environment, Transport and the Regions, Ex p Spath Holme Ltd* [2001] 2 AC 349 House of Lords**

Lord Nicholls: ... Statutory interpretation is an exercise which requires the court to identify the meaning borne by the words in question in the particular context. The task of the court is often said to be to ascertain the intention of Parliament expressed in the language under consideration. This is correct and may be helpful, so long as it is remembered that the 'intention of Parliament' is an objective concept, not subjective. The phrase is a shorthand reference to the intention which the court reasonably imputes to Parliament in respect of the language used. It is not the subjective intention of the minister or other persons who promoted the legislation. Nor is it the subjective intention of the draftsman, or of individual members or even of a majority of individual members of either House. These individuals will often have widely varying intentions. Their understanding of the legislation and the words used may be impressively complete or woefully inadequate. Thus, when courts say that such-and-such a meaning 'cannot be what Parliament intended', they are saying only that the words under consideration cannot reasonably be taken as used by Parliament with that meaning. As Lord Reid said in *Black-Clawson International Ltd v Papierwerke Waldhof-Aschaffenburg AG* [1975] AC 591, 613: 'We often say that we are looking for the intention of Parliament, but that is not quite accurate. We are seeking the meaning of the words which Parliament used.'

In identifying the meaning of the words used, the courts employ accepted principles of interpretation as useful guides. For instance, an appropriate starting point is that language is to be taken to bear its ordinary meaning in the general context of the statute. Another, recently enacted, principle is that so far as possible legislation must be read in a way which is compatible with human rights and fundamental freedoms: see section 3 of the Human Rights Act 1998. The principles of interpretation include also certain presumptions. To take a familiar instance, the courts presume that a mental ingredient is an essential element in every statutory offence unless Parliament has indicated a contrary intention expressly or by necessary implication.

Additionally, the courts employ other recognised aids. They may be internal aids. Other provisions in the same statute may shed light on the meaning of the words under consideration. Or the aids may be external to the statute, such as its background setting and its legislative history. This extraneous material includes reports of Royal Commissions and advisory committees, reports of the Law Commission (with or without a draft Bill attached), and a statute's legislative antecedents.

Use of non-statutory materials as an aid to interpretation is not a new development. As long ago as 1584 the Barons of the Exchequer enunciated the so-called mischief rule. In interpreting statutes courts should take into account, among other matters, 'the mischief and defect for which the common law did not provide': *Heydon's Case* (1584) 3 Co Rep 7a, 7b. Nowadays the courts look at external aids for more than merely identifying the mischief the statute is intended to cure. In adopting a purposive approach to the interpretation of statutory language, courts seek to identify and give effect to the purpose of the legislation. To the extent that extraneous material assists in identifying the purpose of the legislation, it is a useful tool.

This is subject to an important caveat. External aids differ significantly from internal aids. Unlike internal aids, external aids are not found within the statute in which Parliament has expressed its intention in the words in question. This difference is of constitutional importance. Citizens, with the assistance of their advisers, are intended to be able to understand parliamentary enactments, so that they can regulate their conduct accordingly. They should be able to rely upon what they read in an Act of Parliament. This gives rise to a tension between the need for legal certainty, which is one of the fundamental elements of the rule of law, and the need to give effect to the intention of Parliament, from whatever source that (objectively assessed) intention can be gleaned. ...

This constitutional consideration does not mean that when deciding whether statutory language is clear and unambiguous and not productive of absurdity, the courts are confined to looking solely at the language in question in its context within the statute. That would impose on the courts much too restrictive an approach. No legislation is enacted in a vacuum. Regard may also be had to extraneous material, such as the setting in which the legislation was enacted. This is a matter of everyday occurrence.

That said, courts should nevertheless approach the use of external aids with circumspection. Judges frequently turn to external aids for confirmation of views reached without their assistance. That is unobjectionable. But the constitutional implications point to a need for courts to be slow to permit external aids to displace meanings which are otherwise clear and unambiguous and not productive of absurdity. Sometimes external aids may properly operate in this way. In other cases, the requirements of legal certainty might be undermined to an unacceptable extent if the court were to adopt, as the intention to be imputed to Parliament in using the words in question, the meaning suggested by an external aid. Thus, when interpreting statutory language courts have to strike a balance between conflicting considerations.

For some years before 1993 a self-imposed judicial rule precluded use of parliamentary proceedings as an external aid. This exclusionary rule was relaxed by this House in *Pepper v Hart* [1993] AC 593, so as to permit use of parliamentary materials as an aid to construction where certain conditions are satisfied. One of these conditions is that the legislation must be ambiguous or obscure, or lead to an absurdity: see Lord Browne-Wilkinson at p 640.

I can see nothing in this formulation or in principle to suggest that the ambiguity or obscurity or absurdity must be of any particular type. The purpose for which a statutory power is conferred is just as much a question of interpretation of the statutory provision as is the meaning of a particular word or phrase. It cannot be right for the courts to look at parliamentary proceedings, if they assist, on the interpretation of a particular word or phrase, but to decline to look at parliamentary proceedings, however much assistance they may give, when deciding, as a matter of interpretation, what was the purpose for which a power was conferred. The point is underlined by noting that, if drawn, this distinction has the consequence that, in the latter type of case, the courts will look at other forms of extraneous material if they assist, such as statements in Government white papers, but not at what was said by Government ministers in Parliament. This would not be a rational distinction.

Experience has shown that the occasions on which reference to parliamentary proceedings is of assistance are rare. To be of assistance as an external aid, the parliamentary statement relied upon must be clear and unequivocal. Otherwise it is of no real use. Parliamentary statements seldom satisfy this test on the points of interpretation which come before the courts. Increasing awareness of the lack of help provided by parliamentary material will, it is to be hoped, result in counsel being more realistic and more sparing in their references to such material.

As Lord Cooke points out in his speech, this does not mean that the courts will shut out, and not even look at, parliamentary material which one party reasonably contends supports his interpretation of ambiguous legislation. Rather, the courts will consider the material to see whether counsel's contention is well-founded. If the parliamentary statements relied upon are not clear, they are of little or no value and cannot qualify as an external aid in the particular case. They will fail to satisfy the third of Lord Browne-Wilkinson's conditions: see *Pepper v Hart* [1993] AC 593, 640.

If, however, the statements are clear, and were made by a minister or other promoter of the Bill, they qualify as an external aid. In such a case the statements are a factor the court will take into account in construing legislation which is ambiguous or obscure or productive of absurdity. They are then as much part of the background to the legislation as, say, Government white papers. They are part of the legislative background, but they are no more than this. This cannot be emphasised too strongly. Government statements, however they are made and however explicit they may be, cannot control the meaning of an Act of Parliament. As with other extraneous material, it is for the court, when determining what was the intention of Parliament in using the words in question, to decide how much importance, or weight, if any, should be attached to a Government statement. The weight will depend on all the circumstances. For instance, the statement might conflict with the principle of interpretation that penal legislation is to be construed strictly. …

Interpretation in the common law would appear to place much more emphasis on the words of the text (*verba*) than in the civil law (see 1.5 and 1.8). There are historical reasons for this less benign approach; before the 19th century legislation was seen by the judges as somewhat intrusive with respect to the 'purity' of the common law itself. Lord Nicholls also offers certainty as a contemporary reason for a more literal method, although, as he points out, this is now giving way sometimes to a 'purposive' interpretation. Much will depend upon the facts of a case and the circumstances surrounding the application of the statutory provision.

2.6 INTERPRETING CASES

Interpreting legal texts is one thing, but what about legal precedents?

***Woodland v Swimming Teachers Association* [2014] AC 537**
Supreme Court

Lady Hale: ... **28.** The common law is a dynamic instrument. It develops and adapts to meet new situations as they arise. Therein lies its strength. But therein also lies a danger, the danger of unbridled and unprincipled growth to match what the court perceives to be the merits of the particular case. So it must proceed with caution, incrementally by analogy with existing categories, and consistently with some underlying principle (see *Caparo Industries plc v Dickman* [1990] 2 AC 605). But the words used by judges in explaining why they are deciding as they do are not to be treated as if they were the words of statute, setting the rules in stone and precluding further principled development should new situations arise. These things have been said many times before by wiser judges than me, but are worth repeating in this case, where we are accepting an invitation to develop the law beyond the point which it has currently reached in this jurisdiction. It is because we are doing that, and thus disagreeing with the conclusions reached in the courts below, that I am adding a few thoughts to the judgment of Lord Sumption, with which of course I agree.

The approach is thus different. One important difference is this: it must be remembered that it is not the cases themselves that bind but their *rationes decidendi* (*R (Kadim) v Brent Housing Board* [2001] QB 955 para 16).

The Hannah Blumenthal [1983] 1 AC 854 Court of Appeal

Lord Denning MR (Court of Appeal): ... But that raises at once the question: what do you mean by the 'decision' of the higher courts? Presumably the reason for the decision. The ratio decidendi as the classicists call it. The reason which is necessary for the decision. It is binding on the lower courts. It is to be distinguished from the obiter dicta. These are the reasons which are not necessary for the decision. They are not binding on the lower courts. The task of distinguishing between them is formidable. Especially when there are four or five speeches and they each gave different reasons, as in *Boys v Chaplin* [1971] AC 356. Then 'the ratio decidendi of the case must be somewhat speculative': see *Dicey & Morris, The Conflict of Laws*, 10th ed. (1980), vol. 2, p 942; and the lower court can choose which it likes.

To avoid this embarrassment there has been a marked tendency in recent years in the House of Lords for one of their Lordships to give a single speech and the others to concur. The object is, no doubt, to avoid the difficulties caused by different reasons given by different judges. This object is laudable enough. It is much to be commended in some cases. But it is apt to give rise to problems in others.

It may be presumptuous of me to criticise but I make so bold as to indicate to their Lordships the problems to which a single judgment may give rise. Not often, but just occasionally, it makes it exceedingly difficult to discover what is the ratio decidendi of a case – as distinct from the obiter dicta. It is so difficult that often times the lower courts do not even attempt the task. They treat the words of the single judgment as binding authority. They treat them almost as if they were the words of a statute. So treated, the words are apt to lead lower courts astray. Whereas if there had been, not one single judgment, but three or four or five, it would have been much easier to separate the wheat from the chaff and to discover what was really the ratio decidendi – and therefore binding – as distinct from obiter dicta and not binding.

In addition one should recall here Lord Simon's words (in *Lupton v FA & AB Ltd*, above 2.2) that precedent – or more precisely the *ratio decidendi* – is a matter not just of applying a rule distilled from a precedent or line of precedents, but also of comparing by way of analogy the 'material facts' of the precedent with the 'material facts' of the case before the court. This adds a real complication because one has to 'interpret' both the words used by judges in the precedent(s) and the factual situations of these previous cases.

Grant v Australian Knitting Mills Ltd [1936] AC 85 Privy Council

Lord Wright: ... It was argued, but not perhaps very strongly, that *Donoghue's* case was a case of food or drink to be consumed internally, whereas the pants here were to be worn externally. No distinction, however, can be logically drawn for this purpose between a noxious thing taken internally and a noxious thing applied externally: the garments were made to be worn next to the skin: indeed Lord Atkin specifically puts as examples of what is covered by the principle he is enunciating things operating externally, such as 'an ointment, a soap, a cleaning fluid or cleaning powder'. …

This case indicates that it was *not* a material fact in *Donoghue v Stevenson* [1932] AC 562 that the thing that did the damage was a bottle of ginger beer. The relevant fact, at least for the Privy Council in 1936, was 'product'. This permitted what might be seen as a step in an ordered development of the tort of negligence through interpretation.

Can such an interpretative method be seen as something more than just the interpretation of a particular precedent in a particular case?

Knuller Ltd v DPP [1973] AC 435 House of Lords

Lord Simon of Glaisdale: … It is, in general, the difference between mature and rudimentary legal systems that the latter deal specifically with a number of particular and unrelated instances, whereas the former embody the law in comprehensive, cohesive and rational general rules. The law is then easier to understand and commands a greater respect. Fragmentation, on the other hand, leads to anomalous (and therefore inequitable) distinctions and to hedging legal rules round with technicalities that are only within the understanding of an esoteric class. The general development of English law (like that of other mature systems) has been towards the co-ordination of particular instances into comprehensive and comprehensible general rules. The evolution of the compendious tort of negligence from a number of disparate forms of action is a well-known example from the common law: the Theft Act 1968 may be regarded as a statutory counterpart. (I must, however, add the rider that English law has never felt bound to carry every rule to its logical conclusion in the face of convenience.) But the common law proceeds generally by distilling from a particular case the legal principle on which it is decided, and that legal principle is then generally applied to the circumstances of other cases to which the principle is relevant as they arise before the courts. …

This more general and rationalised approach to legal development through interpretation of statute and precedent formed the basis of a legal theory.

Ronald Dworkin, _Law's Empire_, Fontana, 1986, p 229

… We can find an even more fruitful comparison between literature and law … by constructing an artificial genre of literature that we might call the chain novel.

In this enterprise a group of novelists writes a novel *seriatim*; each novelist in the chain interprets the chapters he has been given in order to write a new

> chapter, which is then added to what the next novelist receives, and so on. Each has the job of writing his chapter so as to make the novel being constructed the best it can be, and the complexity of this task models the complexity of deciding a hard case under law as integrity ... In our example ... the novelists are expected to take their responsibilities of continuity ... seriously; they aim jointly to create, so far as they can, a single unified novel that is the best it can be.
>
> He may find, not that no single interpretation fits the bulk of the text, but that more than one does. The second dimension of interpretation then requires him to judge which of these eligible readings makes the work in progress best, all things considered. At this point his more substantive aesthetic judgments, about the importance or insight or realism or beauty of different ideas the novel might be taken to express, come into play ...

The importance of Dworkin's work lies in his emphasis on judge and judging. Such a person is at the heart of his legal theory; law itself is interpretation (see 2.3). Furthermore, for Dworkin, there is always a right answer to any hard case and thus he rejected the idea that when faced with an ambiguous statutory word or phrase or a precedent the judge has discretion. Of course, such a right answer – based on the idea that law is a matter of argumentation and that there is always one argument that is superior to all others – might well be beyond the capacity of a human judge. Dworkin thus created a superhuman judge (Hercules) that he employed when discussing his interpretative model. There is, then, an element of fiction in Dworkin's depiction of legal interpretation. However it could be argued that all theories of judging incorporate fiction at some level. Are not all legal categories, concepts and theories fictional creations in the sense that they create 'as if' models? Do not lawyers, and those under their influence, behave 'as if' there is such a thing as contract, ownership and the like? This is a question to which we will return (see 6.8).

FURTHER READING AND QUESTIONS

1. On policy reasoning and also Dworkin see Bell (1983). Most general textbooks on the English legal system will have chapters on statutory interpretation and case law reasoning. Two key works on legal reasoning are MacCormick (1978) and (2005). Another very useful work is Twining and Miers (2010). On statutory interpretation see Duxbury (2013).
2. Are all legal rules basically the same or are there different types of rules? For example, are there some rules that can be applied syllogistically while there are others that cannot?

3. Should a distinction be made between rules and principles? If so, what is the basis of the distinction?
4. It is the will (*voluntas*) not the words (*verba*) of the legislator that the interpreter of legislation has to seek, said Hugues Doneau (*voluntas haec ex fine iuris colligitur*) (*Commentarii de jure civili*, book 1, chap 13, § 12). For words without purpose are not statute law (*verba autem sine sentential legis ius non sunt*) (*ibid*, § 13). Does this principle apply to English law?
5. Doneau also asserted that legislative rationality (*rationem legis*), will (*voluntas*) and purpose (*sententia legis*) should be seen as all coming together in legislation (*ibid*, chap 14, § 6). Do English judges take the same view? (Cf Duxbury, 2013.)

3. Judging and legal reasoning today ('official portrait') (2)

In the last chapter we saw how the legal philosopher Ronald Dworkin developed a theory of law based upon interpretation. The role of the judge is one of interpreter. Dworkin is also known for his other major contribution to a theory of law and legal reasoning: that judges should concern themselves only with the determination of people's rights.

3.1 RIGHTS MODEL

The idea of law as rights was by no means invented by Dworkin. Indeed some argue that its foundation is in the word *ius*, which in later Roman law appeared to have had a sense close to that of a 'right'. The word *ius* was certainly given this sense by later continental jurists.

Justinian, *Institutes*, Book 4, Title 6, preface (also *Digest* 44.7.51)

An action (*actio*) is nothing other than a right (*ius*) to sue for what is owed to one.

But Dworkin developed this rights model in order to set out the role of the judge in the common law world.

R Dworkin, *Taking Rights Seriously*, Duckworth, 1977, pp 85, 87, 101, 116–117

But suppose … that a judge successfully justifies a decision in a hard case … on grounds not of policy but of principle. Suppose, that is, that he is able to show that the plaintiff has a *right* to recover… damages. The rights thesis … provides a more satisfactory explanation of how judges use precedent in hard cases than the explanation provided by any theory that gives a more prominent place to policy. The rights thesis provides that judges decide hard cases by confirming or denying concrete rights. [The superhuman judge] must construct a scheme of abstract and concrete principles that provides a coherent justification for all common law precedents and, so far as these are to be justified on principle, constitutional and statutory provisions as well.

Yet what exactly is meant by the term 'right'?

Geoffrey Samuel, *Law of Obligations and Legal Remedies*, Cavendish, 2nd ed, 2001, p 89 (footnotes omitted)

A legal right … is a construct of legal science: it takes its form from the relationship between *persona* and *res* and this is the reason why one always talks of a right to something. In other words a right is a legal concept that uses the conceptual structure of the property relationship between person and thing and applies it to other legal (and indeed political and social) relationships. Thus performance under a contract can be seen as a *res* to which the other contracting party (*persona*) is entitled and this leads to a situation where one can talk in terms of a right arising from a contract. …

What is being asserted here is a structural view of a 'right'. It is an abstract notion based on a relationship between two institutional elements of a person and a thing. However this structural definition does not really capture the differing intensities that can attach to the concept.

***In re KD (a minor)* [1988] 1 AC 806 House of Lords**

Lord Oliver: … The word 'right' is used in a variety of different senses, both popular and jurisprudential. It may be used as importing a positive duty in some other individual for the non-performance of which the law will provide an appropriate remedy, as in the case of a right to the performance of a contract. It may signify merely a privilege conferring no corresponding duty on any one save that of non-interference, such as the right to walk on the public highway. It may signify no more than the hope of or aspiration to a social order which will permit the exercise of that which is perceived as an essential liberty, such as, for instance, the so-called 'right to work' or a 'right' of personal privacy.

Yet even if one could better define a right, would this be enough?

Steve Hedley, Looking Outward or Looking Inward? Obligations Scholarship in the Early 21st Century, in Andrew Robertson and Tang Hang Wu (eds), *The Goals of Private Law*, Hart, 2009, p 196 (footnotes omitted)

Rights Theorists regard the key question in obligations cases as the identification of the plaintiff's right, arguing that once this is done, the answer to other questions should fall into place rapidly and uncontroversially. In particular, this minimises reference to policy concerns, which are seen as objectionable. 'Name the right, define it, and the rest is mere application in the light of the circumstances. More juris, less prudence' ... A notable feature of the theory is the reluctance, to date, to definitively list the rights, or describe them in other than vague terms.

There is, then, an ambiguity that attaches to the notion of a right. One problem is that a range of rather different legal claims can all attract the term right. For example, if one enters a free public car park one can talk of one's 'right' to park there. However is this 'right' as strong as the one where a person might have paid a yearly subscription to park his car in a particular reserved space in a car park? The jurist Wesley Hohfeld (1879–1918) fashioned a structural framework whereby a 'right' (for example where one had contracted to park) was distinguished from a mere 'liberty' (for example to park one's car in a public car park), with the former having a co-relative of a 'duty' (Hohfeld, 1919). So one only has a right where there exists a co-relative duty. However this structure does not always work because 'duty' can also be ambiguous. Yet, despite the ambiguity with regard to the definition of a right, it can prove a useful reasoning tool.

***Ex parte Island Records* [1978] Ch 122 Court of Appeal**

Lord Denning MR: ... The question ... becomes this: has the plaintiff a particular right which he is entitled to have protected? To this the answer which runs through all the cases is: a man who is carrying on a lawful trade or calling has a right to be protected from any unlawful interference with it ... It is a right which is in the nature of a right of property ... [The Attorney-General] has, we are told, refused his consent to a relator action – presumably because no public rights are involved. So perforce if the law is to be obeyed – and justice to be done – the courts must allow a private individual himself to bring an action against the offender – in those cases where his private rights and interests are specially affected by the breach [of the criminal law]. This principle is capable of extension so as to apply not only to rights of property or rights in the nature of it, but to other rights or interests. ...

Rights-reasoning is, it would seem, also central to issues of human rights, especially now that the UK has incorporated the European Convention on Human Rights directly into its law (Human Rights Act 1998). Yet the actual reasoning concerning 'rights' proves more complex than Lord Denning's approach might suggest.

***Wilson v First County Trust Ltd (No 2)* [2004] 1 AC 816 House of Lords**

Lord Rodger: ... **179** The 1998 Act is beautifully drafted. Its structure is tight and elegant, being marred only by the obvious interpolation of sections 12 and 13 as a result of amendments made while the Bill was passing through Parliament. The presence or absence of particular features in the Act is therefore unlikely to be due to oversight.

181 It is well recognised ... that Convention rights are to be seen as an expression of fundamental principles rather than as a set of mere rules. In applying the principles the courts must balance competing interests. Therefore, when deciding whether the order sought by one private party would infringe a Convention right of the other, a court must balance the interests of both parties. If the court finds that the order would infringe the Convention right of the party against whom it would be made, this can only be because the court has concluded that his interests are to be preferred to any competing interests of the party seeking the order. In particular, the court must have concluded that the Convention right of the party resisting the order is to be preferred to the other party's common law or statutory right to obtain it.

182 The 1998 Act is unusual – perhaps unique – in its range. While most statutes apply to one particular topic or area of law, the 1998 Act works as a catalyst across the board, wherever a Convention right is engaged. It may affect matters of substance in such areas as the law of property, the law of marriage and the law of torts. Or else it may affect civil and criminal procedure, or the procedure of administrative tribunals.

We shall see that the notion of an 'interest' is capable of acting in itself as the basis of a reasoning model (see 3.4). However it equally acts as a restraining element to the notion of a right in that it becomes a mediating factor when two apparent rights conflict (for example the right to reputation conflicts with the right to publish). Lord Rodger also describes the Convention 'rights' as fundamental 'principles'. Is principle just a right seen from a different perspective or do all rights derive from principles? The question is an important one in terms of the rights model because the idea of case law as a set of principles derived from the precedents seems now to be embedded in English legal thinking.

Practice Direction (Citation of Authorities) [2012] 1 WLR 780

10 ... An unreported case should not usually be cited unless it contains a relevant statement of legal principle not found in reported authority.

It does not follow of course that legal principle is the basis of a rights model of law. A principle is simply a rule (*regula iuris*) at a high level of abstraction and thus can be seen as an aspect of the rule model (cf 2.1).

3.2 ABUSE OF RIGHTS

However are there principles that might defeat the exercise of a right? In the civil law there is the principle of an abuse of a right whereby a person who exercises a right in an abusive manner will be subject to a legal sanction. Is such a principle to be found in English law?

Bradford Corporation v Pickles [1895] AC 587 House of Lords

Lord Halsbury LC: ... The only remaining point is the question of fact alleged by the plaintiffs, that the acts done by the defendant are done, not with any view which deals with the use of his own land or the percolating water through it, but is done, in the language of the pleader, 'maliciously' ...

This is not a case in which the state of mind of the person doing the act can affect the right to do it. If it was a lawful act, however ill the motive might be, he had a right to do it. If it was an unlawful act, however good his motive might be, he would have no right to do it ...

Lord Macnaghten: ... But the real answer to the claim of the corporation is that in such a case motives are immaterial. It is the act, not the motive for the act, that must be regarded. If the act, apart from motive, gives rise merely to damage without legal injury, the motive, however reprehensible it may be, will not supply that element ...

If this case had arisen in France it is quite possible that the defendant would have been held liable for abusing his property right. In English law it would seem, in contrast, that rights are absolute. Yet care must be taken here because rights-thinking is not the only type of reasoning employed by common law judges; there are many cases where 'unreasonable' behaviour by an apparent right holder has been sanctioned by a legal remedy. Sometimes it depends on how the facts are perceived and categorised (see eg *Ruxley Electronics Ltd v Forsyth* [1996] 1 AC 344); at other times it is a matter of extending a cause of action to cover the abusive behaviour in issue (see eg *Hollywood Silver Fox Farm v Emmett* [1936] 2 KB 468). Much depends upon whether one puts the emphasis on the right or on the unreasonable behaviour.

3.3 POLICY MODEL

Dworkin developed his rights model in part as a reaction to reasoning by reference to policy. In order to understand this distinction it must be recalled that the models discussed so far can be described as formalist intellectual constructions. That is to say they are reasoning models that are founded upon systems of thought that do not aim to describe social reality as such. They are coherent systems of rules and (or) rights that inhabit their own intellectual sphere in which the coherence of the system, rather than reflection of reality, provides the epistemological (knowledge) validation. In contrast to such formalist (or idealist) constructions are models that aim to reflect social reality of which the most important, for judging purposes, is policy reasoning. This kind of reasoning is best described as functional; that is to say the reasoning is of a kind that emphasises the function of a legal rule or concept and measures the efficiency of the rule to this function.

***Spartan Steel & Alloys Ltd v Martin & Co (Contractors) Ltd* [1973] 1 QB 27 Court of Appeal**

Lord Denning MR: ... At bottom I think the question of recovering economic loss is one of policy. Whenever the courts draw a line to mark out the bounds of duty, they do it as matter of policy so as to limit the responsibility of the defendant. Whenever the courts set bounds to the damages recoverable – saying that they are, or are not, too remote – they do it as matter of policy so as to limit the liability of the defendant. ...

The second consideration is the nature of the hazard, namely, the cutting of the supply of electricity. This is a hazard which we all run. It may be due to a short circuit, to a flash of lightning, to a tree falling on the wires, to an accidental cutting of the cable, or even to the negligence of someone or other. And when it does happen, it affects a multitude of persons; not as a rule by way of physical damage to them or their property, but by putting them to inconvenience, and sometimes to economic loss. The supply is usually restored in a few hours, so the economic loss is not very large. Such a hazard is regarded by most people as a thing they must put up with – without seeking compensation from anyone. Some there are who install a stand-by system. Others seek refuge by taking out an insurance policy against breakdown in the supply. But most people are content to take the risk on themselves. When the supply is cut off, they do not go running round to their solicitor. They do not try to find out whether it was anyone's fault. They just put up with it. They try to make up the economic loss by doing more work next day. This is a healthy attitude which the law should encourage.

According to Lord Denning one of the functions of the economic loss rule in the tort of negligence is its purpose of limiting claims – to discourage people who suffer just economic loss from 'running round to their solicitor'. This, he said, is a 'healthy attitude'. This may seem a much more 'common sense' approach to legal reasoning.

> ***Ex parte King* [1984] 3 All ER 897 Court of Appeal**
>
> **Griffiths LJ**: ... [T]he common law of England has not always developed on strictly logical lines, and where logic leads down a path that is beset with practical difficulties the courts have not been frightened to turn aside and seek the pragmatic solution that will best serve the needs of society.

As for 'policy' itself, it has been defined, or at least described, as something beyond the purely legal.

> ***D v NSPCC* [1978] AC 171 House of Lords**
>
> **Lord Simon**: ... Of course, every rule of law is a legal manifestation of public policy. But your Lordships are ... instantly concerned with 'public policy' in a narrower sense – namely, consideration of social interests beyond the purely legal which call for the modification of a normal legal rule ...

Yet policy reasoning can create its own particular problems. The first is that judges can disagree as to the policy.

> ***Barclays Bank v O'Brien* [1992] 3 WLR 593 Court of Appeal**
> **[1994] 1 AC 180 House of Lords**
>
> **Scott LJ** (Court of Appeal): ... These authorities seem to me to leave the developing law, if not at the crossroads, at least at the junction of two diverging roads ... The choice between the two roads cannot, in my opinion, be made simply by reference to binding authority. Binding authority can be found to justify either. The choice should, I think, be a matter of policy. Ought the law to treat married women who provide security for their husband's debts, and others in an analogous position, as requiring special protection? The position of married women today, both generally and vis-à-vis their husbands is very different from what it was ... But ... in the culturally and ethnically mixed community in which we live, the degree of emancipation of women is uneven.
>
> **Lord Browne-Wilkinson** (House of Lords): ... On the other hand, it is important to keep a sense of balance in approaching these cases. It is easy to allow sympathy for the wife who is threatened with the loss of her home at the suit of a rich bank to obscure an important public interest viz, the need to ensure that

> the wealth currently tied up in the matrimonial home does not become economically sterile. If the rights secured to wives by the law renders vulnerable loans granted on the security of matrimonial homes, institutions will be unwilling to accept such security, thereby reducing the flow of loan capital to business enterprises. It is therefore essential that a law designed to protect the vulnerable does not render the matrimonial home unacceptable as security to financial institutions.

The second problem is one of research. No competent social scientist would make assertions about social reality without basing them on proper empirical research. Judges, however, do not seem to feel the need to undertake such research when they have recourse to the policy model of reasoning.

> ***Crawford Adjusters (Cayman) Ltd v Sagicor General Insurance (Cayman) Ltd* [2013] 3 WLR 927 Privy Council**
>
> **Lord Kerr**: ... **94.** ... As a general observation, however, it is right to recognise that conclusions on matters of policy in the legal context are not usually the product of empirical research. Customarily, they are formed instinctually and constitute, at most, informed guesswork about the impact that the selection of a particular policy course will have. While, therefore, policy considerations can, and on occasions must, underlie decisions as to how law should develop, it is necessary to recognise the inherent impossibility of making an infallible prediction about the outcome of a policy choice. Where possible, therefore, such a choice should be aligned with principle. In my view, fundamental principle has a large part to play in the resolution of the debate in this case. And the pre-eminent principle at stake here is that for every injustice there should be remedy at law.

Ronald Dworkin insisted on a difference between principle and policy and argued that judges should concern themselves only with the former. In other words Dworkin was an idealist rather than a realist. Yet where Dworkin has a point is with regard to this lack of any empirical social science research; judges often seem to indulge in 'armchair' sociology (see *Elguzouli-Daf* below). Nevertheless, others have convincingly shown that when it comes to the reasoning of common law judges the distinction between principle and policy makes no sense; the principles formulated by the judges usually have within them a functional or policy dimension (see eg Waddams, 2011). Whatever the situation there is little doubt that the policy model of reasoning is well embedded into judicial reasoning and so it is unlikely that realism will be completely abandoned by the courts.

***Elguzouli-Daf v Commissioner of Police of the Metropolis* [1995] QB 335 Court of Appeal**

Steyn LJ: ... That brings me to the policy factors which, in my view, argue against the recognition of a duty of care owed by the CPS to those it prosecutes. While it is always tempting to yield to an argument based on the protection of civil liberties, I have come to the conclusion that the interests of the whole community are better served by not imposing a duty of care on the CPS. In my view, such a duty of care would tend to have an inhibiting effect on the discharge by the CPS of its central function of prosecuting crime. It would in some cases lead to a defensive approach by prosecutors to their multifarious duties. It would introduce a risk that prosecutors would act so as to protect themselves from claims of negligence. The CPS would have to spend valuable time and use scarce resources in order to prevent law suits in negligence against the CPS. It would generate a great deal of paper to guard against the risks of law suits. The time and energy of CPS lawyers would be diverted from concentrating on their prime function of prosecuting offenders. That would be likely to happen not only during the prosecution process but also when the CPS is sued in negligence by aggrieved defendants. The CPS would be constantly enmeshed in an avalanche of interlocutory civil proceedings and civil trials. That is a spectre that would bode ill for the efficiency of the CPS and the quality of our criminal justice system.

This policy approach has again been confirmed by the Supreme Court, but with some recognition towards Dworkin's view that policy ought to be a matter for the legislature.

***Michael v Chief Constable of South Wales Police* [2015] UKSC 2 Supreme Court**

Lord Toulson: ... **102.** It is true that the categories of negligence are never closed (*Heaven v Pender* (1883) 11 QBD 503), and it would be open to the court to create a new exception to the general rule about omissions. The development of the law of negligence has been by an incremental process rather than giant steps. The established method of the court involves examining the decided cases to see how far the law has gone and where it has refrained from going. From that analysis it looks to see whether there is an argument by analogy for extending liability to a new situation, or whether an earlier limitation is no longer logically or socially justifiable. In doing so it pays regard to the need for overall coherence. Often there will be a mixture of policy considerations to take into account. ...

107. The *Anns* formula was finally disapproved in *Murphy v Brentwood District Council* [1991] AC 398. The particular question in that case was whether the owner of a house built with defective foundations was owed a duty of care by the local authority which passed the plans. The House of Lords held that he was not. The property was the plaintiff's home and it would have cost more than half of its value in good condition to repair the damage caused by the defective foundations. Lord Bridge observed that there might be cogent reasons of social policy for imposing liability on the authority, but that the shoulders of a public authority were only broad enough to bear the loss because they were financed by the public at large, and that it was pre-eminently a matter for the legislature whether these policy reasons should be accepted as sufficient for imposing on the public the burden of providing compensation for the plaintiff's private loss. Similarly Lord Oliver said that it would not be right for the courts to create new principles in order to fulfil a social need in an area of consumer protection where there was legislation.

This observation by Lord Toulson would appear to confirm Professor Waddams' account of judicial reasoning in as much as it is indicating that making a strict distinction between policy and principle is not always easy or viable. Equally, however, it is recognising that a distinction can sometimes be made between a matter of principle and a matter of policy. Recently the Supreme Court has warned against policy being used as an excuse for the exercise of discretion.

Jetiva SA v Bilta (UK) Ltd [2015] UKSC 23 Supreme Court

Lord Sumption: … **99.** Given that the illegality defence is based on public policy, it is understandable that policy should have been invoked in a number of academic and judicial analyses of these problems. It is, however, important to bear in mind the proper role of policy in the law of illegality, for arguments based upon it can easily degenerate into the kind of discretionary weighing of the equities which was rejected in *Tinsley v Milligan* and *Les Laboratoires Servier v Apotex Inc.* The fact that the illegality defence is based on policy does not entitle a court to reassess the value or relevance of that policy on a case-by-case basis. In a broad sense, any rule of law which imposes civil liability in respect of a wrong may be described as a reflection of legal policy. It does not follow that the courts may apply the illegality defence or not according to the relative importance which they attach to the policy underlying it by comparison with desirability of allowing an otherwise sound claim to succeed. This was the essential problem about the reasoning of the Court of Appeal in *Les Laboratoires Servier*, which explains why this court felt unable to adopt that reasoning while arriving at the same result.

Admittedly Lord Sumption is talking about policy in regard to the defence of illegality, but his words probably have a wider application and might thus be relevant for policy arguments in general.

3.4 INTEREST MODEL

If one had to find a legal concept that lies midway between the rights model and the policy model it would be the notion of an interest.

Geoffrey Samuel, The Notion of an Interest as a Formal Concept in English and in Comparative Law, in G Canivet, M Andenas and D Fairgrieve (eds), *Comparative Law Before the Courts*, 2004, British Institute of International and Comparative Law, 262, pp 262–263
(footnotes omitted)

There are a range of reasons why an 'interest' deserves analysis by a comparative lawyer. The notion of an interest is by its very nature one of the most central of all legal concepts since it is one that, like the legal subject (*persona*) or the legal objects (*res*), exists at one and the same time in both the legal world and the world of social reality. It is, in other words, a truly mediating concept between fact and law. Secondly, it is a notion that goes back to Roman times and thus is a legal concept that should attract the attention of the legal theorist specialising in epistemology and the comparative lawyer. Equally, and this is a third reason, it is a concept that connects with what must be the most famous of legal notions, that of a 'right'. An interest often appears to be a kind of halfway house between a right and a remedy. The notion of an interest is, accordingly, a useful starting point for examining a range of other conceptual concepts. Fourthly, an interest is a notion that connects with the *persona* (legal subject) as an individual: to determine an interest, is to determine a legal subject and his, her or its expectations. An interest, then, is a legal concept that can play a central role in legal thought and legal reasoning; it is a 'passport' to all areas of the law. Fifthly, in having its basic roots in the world of fact rather than in the normative abstraction of law, it is a concept that would appear to lie beyond the rule. It is a concept that, itself, suggests that legal knowledge is not exclusively rule-based. Indeed, this factual dimension to the notion of an interest allows it to be used as the basis of an 'actional' scheme of intelligibility: thus in economics it represents the self-interested actor. Because such an actor also has a role in the legal plan, the notion of an interest can act as a link between law and another discipline such as economics. Finally, therefore, the notion of an interest is a key means by which one can understand legal reasoning. It bridges the gap not just between legal substance and legal method, but equally between judgment and solution; it is the means by which one can have access to the thinking that lies behind the more formal elements of legal knowledge, that is to say behind rules and legal rights. It is, in brief, a key to legal knowledge.

This notion of an interest has been the subject of a detailed and seminal analysis by a leading Belgian jurist who was one of the first to describe it as a 'passport' to all areas of the law (Ost, 1990). Professor Ost's monograph deals with the civil law, but what makes the notion of an interest rather complex in English law is that 'interest' can mean different things in different contexts.

Peter Cane, *Tort Law and Economic Interests*, Oxford University Press, 2nd ed, 1996, pp 3–4

... In the first place, it is worth noting some nuances in the use of the word 'interest'. When we speak of someone having, for instance, a 'property interest', we mean that the person has some sort of claim over or right in some tangible or intangible thing; and when we speak of someone having a 'contractual interest' we mean that the person has some claim or right by reason of a contract. In such instances the word 'interest' is more or less synonymous with the words 'right' or 'claim'. An interest in this sense relates to (or is 'in' or 'over') some tangible or intangible thing such as property or contract. A useful general term to describe the subject matter of interests is 'assets' ... On the other hand, we often speak of a person's interests or of the public interest in a broader sense to mean simply objectives or states of affairs which are, or would be, to the person's or the public's advantage: for example, the public interest in the due administration of justice, thought to be furthered by the barrister's [former] immunity from suit in respect of negligence in the conduct of litigation in court; or the interest in free competition recognized in the defence of justification in the tort of conspiracy ... While it is clear that both types of interest may be 'legal' in the sense of 'recognized and protected by law', interests of the former type are, on the whole, better protected than those of the latter type, at least in the sense that interests of the former type often constitute legal 'swords', whereas those of the latter type are often only effective as 'shields'.

In terms of actual legal reasoning the notion of an interest often plays a mediating role between law and fact.

Tony Weir, *A Casebook on Tort*, Sweet & Maxwell, 9th ed, 2000, p 6

To cause harm means to have an adverse effect on something good. There are several good things in life, such as liberty, bodily integrity, land, possessions, reputation, wealth, privacy, dignity, perhaps even life itself. Lawyers call these goods 'interests.' These interests are all good, but they are not all *equally* good. This is evident when they come into conflict (one may jettison cargo to save passengers, but not vice versa, and one may detain a thing, but not a person, as security for a debt). Because these interests are not equally good, the protection afforded to them by the law is not equal; the law protects the better interests better: murder and rape are, after all, more serious crimes than theft. Accordingly, the better the interest invaded, the more readily does the law give compensation for the ensuing harm.

Tony Weir, *A Casebook on Tort*, Sweet & Maxwell, 1967, p 3

Midway in abstraction between 'right' and 'damage' comes 'interest.' Perhaps the relationship can be put this way: all rights, however infringed, involve liability; all legally protected interests, relevantly infringed, involve liability; but some damage (eg grief), however produced, does not involve liability.

Interest can link 'damage' (or 'harm') in the world of social reality to 'damage' or 'harm' in the legal world. Thus a person who suffers only pure economic loss or mental distress as a result of the defendant's negligence is often said to have an unprotected interest. In other words the law will not treat these forms of harm as legal 'damage' for the purposes of the tort of negligence. Although there is a normative implication in this damage-as-interest meaning, the notion is essentially descriptive. It is not like the notion of a 'right', which implies a legal entitlement.

This said, there are occasions when an interest has been used in this more active sense.

***Beswick v Beswick* [1966] Ch 538 Court of Appeal**

Lord Denning MR: ... The general rule undoubtedly is that 'no third person can sue, or be sued, on a contract to which he is not a party'; but at bottom that is only a rule of procedure. It goes to the form of remedy, not to the underlying right. Where a contract is made for the benefit of a third person who has a legitimate interest to enforce it, it can be enforced by the third party in the name of the contracting party or jointly with him or, if he refuses to join, by adding him as a defendant. In that sense, and it is a very real sense, the third person has a right arising by way of contract. He has an interest which will be protected by law ... It is different when a third person has no legitimate interest, as when ... he is seeking to rely, not on any right given to him by the contract, but on an exemption clause ...

Lord Denning here is careful not to treat an interest as if it is a right. What he does is to recognise the interest as empirically existing and then he asserts that it can be given legal expression indirectly (for example using the name of the actual contracting party).

Sometimes, however, an interest can act as a more direct basis for the granting of a legal remedy.

***Burris v Azadani* [1995] 1 WLR 1372 Court of Appeal**

Sir Thomas Bingham MR: ... Neither statute nor authority in my view precludes the making of an 'exclusion zone' order. But that does not mean that such orders should be made at all readily, or without very good reason. There are two interests to be reconciled. One is that of the defendant. His liberty must be respected up to the point at which his conduct infringes, or threatens to infringe, the rights of the plaintiff. No restraint should be placed on him which is not judged to be necessary to protect the rights of the plaintiff. But the plaintiff has an interest which the court must be astute to protect. The rule of law requires that those whose rights are infringed should seek the aid of the court, and respect for the legal process can only suffer if those who need protection fail to get it. That, in part at least, is why disobedience to orders of the court has always earned severe punishment. Respect for the freedom of the aggressor should never lead the court to deny necessary protection to the victim.

Schiemann LJ: I agree with the judgment delivered by Sir Thomas Bingham MR. As he points out, there are in these cases two interests to be reconciled – that of the plaintiff not to be harassed and that of the defendant to be allowed to move freely along the highway. An exclusion zone order interferes with the latter in order to secure the former. On its face it forbids what are lawful actions. The defendant has rendered himself liable to such an order because of his previous harassing behaviour. Nonetheless a judge imposing such an order must be careful not to interfere with the defendant's rights more than is necessary in order to protect the plaintiff's.

The judges seem to be treating an interest in this case 'as if' it is some sort of right; and Sir Thomas Bingham invokes respect for the law as justification. One might note that what is in issue here is a conflict between the public and the private. The defendant has a public interest 'right' to move along the highway freely while the claimant has a private right not to be harassed. This public and private dichotomy can be used as the basis for refusing a remedy.

***Miller v Jackson* [1977] QB 966 Court of Appeal**

Lord Denning MR: ... This case is new. It should be approached on principles applicable to modern conditions. There is a contest here between the interest of the public at large and the interest of a private individual. The *public* interest lies in protecting the environment by preserving our playing fields in the face of mounting development, and by enabling our youth to enjoy all the benefits of outdoor games, such as cricket and football. The *private* interest lies in securing the privacy of his home and garden without intrusion or interference by anyone. In deciding between these two conflicting interests, it must be remembered that it is not a question of damages. If by a million-to-one chance a cricket ball does go out of the ground and cause damage, the cricket club will pay. There is no difficulty on that score. No, it is a question of an injunction. And in our law you will find it repeatedly affirmed that an injunction is a discretionary remedy. In a new situation like this, we have to think afresh as to how discretion should be exercised ... As between their conflicting interests, I am of opinion that the public interest should prevail over the private interest ...

Cumming-Bruce LJ: ... With all respect, in my view the learned judge ... does not appear to have had regard to the interest of the inhabitants of the village as a whole. Had he done so he would in my view have been led to the conclusion that the plaintiffs having accepted the benefit of the open space marching with their land should accept the restrictions on enjoyment of their garden which they may reasonably think necessary. There are here special circumstances which should inhibit a court of equity from granting the injunction claimed ...

Normally an owner of property has the right to the peaceful use and enjoyment of his or her land. However the two judges in this case are saying that this right can be subject to limitation where the public interest is in issue. An interest can, it would seem, limit the scope of a right, perhaps reducing this 'right' to little more than an enforceable interest.

3.5 REMEDIES MODEL

The rights model of legal reasoning gives expression to a celebrated maxim: *ubi ius ibi remedium* (where there is a right there is a remedy). Thus if D invades C's right, C is automatically entitled to a legal remedy. Rights, however, are normally associated with mature legal systems. Both the Roman and the English legal systems, in their early centuries, seemed to reflect a reversal of the *ubi ius* maxim: *ubi remedium ibi ius* (where there is a remedy there is a right). Indeed Roman law never really abandoned its actions approach and, it would seem, nor has the common law.

Davy v Spelthorne BC [1984] AC 262 House of Lords

Lord Wilberforce: ... The expressions 'private law' and 'public law' have recently been imported into the law of England from countries which, unlike our own, have separate systems concerning public law and private law. No doubt they are convenient expressions for descriptive purposes. In this country they must be used with caution, for, typically, English law fastens not on principles but on remedies. The principle remains intact that public authorities and public servants are, unless clearly exempted, answerable in the ordinary courts for wrongs done to individuals.

This remedies approach is in turn linked to the existence of a 'cause of action'.

> ***Kingdom of Spain v Christie, Mason & Woods Ltd* [1986] 1 WLR 1120 Chancery Division**
>
> **Sir Nicholas Browne-Wilkinson VC**: ... Therefore, says Mr Littman, he is entitled in this case to a declaration of the falsity of the documents, there being a general right to restrain the circulation of untrue statements. He has shown a basic right and therefore is entitled to a declaration to the effect that the documents are untrue. I was unpersuaded by that analysis. In the pragmatic way in which English law has developed, a man's legal rights are in fact those which are protected by a cause of action. It is not in accordance, as I understand it, with the principles of English law to analyse rights as being something separate from the remedy given to the individual.

But what, exactly, is a 'cause of action'?

> ***Letang v Cooper* [1965] 1 QB 232 Court of Appeal**
>
> **Diplock LJ**: ... A cause of action is simply a factual situation the existence of which entitles one person to obtain from the court a remedy against another person. Historically, the means by which the remedy was obtained varied with the nature of the factual situation and causes of action were divided into categories according to the 'form of action' by which the remedy was obtained in the particular kind of factual situation which constituted the cause of action. But that is legal history, not current law ... The Judicature Act, 1873 abolished forms of action. It did not affect causes of action; so it was convenient for lawyers and legislators to continue to use, to describe the various categories of factual situations which entitle one person to obtain from the court a remedy against another, the names of the various 'forms of action' by which formerly the remedy appropriate to the particular category of factual situation was obtained. But it is essential to realise that when, since 1873, the name of a form of action is used to identify a cause of action, it is used as a convenient and succinct description of a particular category of factual situation which entitles one person to obtain from the court a remedy against another person. To forget this will indeed encourage the old forms of action to rule us from their graves.

The 'forms of action' thinking arose from the medieval common law where, in order to be able to sue in one of the common law courts, the claimant had to purchase the correct form of writ.

RC van Caenegem, History of European Civil Procedure, *International Encyclopedia of Comparative Law*, Volume XVI, Chapter 2 (1973)

22. *The Rise of the Writ System.* – The system of forms of action or the writ system, rightly considered as the most important characteristic of English medieval law, was not abolished until the nineteenth century.

The choice of the action had to be made at the outset by the plaintiff and there was nothing haphazard about it. Litigants who sued by the wrong form of action were in mercy for a false claim and must purchase another writ. If a plaintiff had several alternative forms of action, he must take them in their proper order and the same rule applied to the various steps to be taken in an action. The plaintiff whose statement of claim (or count, *narratio*) departed in even the smallest degree from his writ at once lost his action.

Diplock LJ's reference to the forms of action ruling from their graves was a reference to a famous quote made by FW Maitland.

FW Maitland, *The Forms of Action at Common Law*, Cambridge University Press, Reprint 1979 (first published 1909), p 1

What was a form of action? Already owing to modern reforms it is impossible to assume that every law student must have heard or read or discovered for himself an answer to that question, but it is still one which must be answered if he is to have more than a very superficial knowledge of our law as it stands even at the present day [ie in 1909]. The forms of action we have buried, but they still rule us from their graves. ...

Even half a century after Maitland, his observation still had a ring of truth.

***Esso Petroleum Co Ltd v Southport Corporation* [1954] 2 QB 182 Court of Appeal**

Denning LJ (Court of Appeal): This is one of those cases, rare nowadays, where much depends on ascertaining the proper cause of action, particularly with regard to the burden of proof. The judge seems to have thought that it did not matter much what was the proper cause of action; it all came back in the end to the universal tort of negligence. I do not share this view.

(1) *Trespass to land.* I am clearly of opinion that the Southport Corporation cannot here sue in trespass. This discharge of oil was not done directly on to their foreshore, but outside in the estuary. It was carried by the tide on to their land, but that was only consequential, not direct. Trespass, therefore, does not lie.

(2) *Private nuisance.* In order to support an action on the case for a private nuisance the defendant must have used his own land or some other land in such

a way as injuriously to affect the enjoyment of the plaintiffs' land. 'The ground of responsibility,' said Lord Wright in *Sedleigh-Denfield v. O'Callaghan*, 'is the possession and control of the land from which the nuisance proceeds.' Applying this principle, it is clear that the discharge of oil was not a private nuisance, because it did not involve the use by the defendants of any land, but only of a ship at sea.

(3) *Public nuisance.* The term 'public nuisance' covers a multitude of sins, great and small. Suffice it to say that the discharge of a noxious substance in such a way as to be likely to affect the comfort and safety of Her Majesty's subjects generally is a public nuisance.

Applying the old cases to modern instances, it is, in my opinion, a public nuisance to discharge oil into the sea in such circumstances that it is likely to be carried on to the shores and beaches of our land to the prejudice and discomfort of Her Majesty's subjects. It is an offence punishable by the common law. Furthermore, if any person should suffer greater damage or inconvenience from the oil than the generality of the public, he can have an action to recover damages on that account, provided, of course, that he can discover the offender who discharged the oil. This action would have been described in the old days as an action on the case, but it is now simply an action for a nuisance.

(4) *Burden of proof.* One of the principal differences between an action for a public nuisance and an action for negligence is the burden of proof. In an action for a public nuisance, once the nuisance is proved and the defendant is shown to have caused it, then the legal burden is shifted on to the defendant to justify or excuse himself. If he fails to do so, he is held liable, whereas in an action for negligence the legal burden in most cases remains throughout on the plaintiff. In negligence, the plaintiff may gain much help from provisional presumptions like the doctrine of *res ipsa loquitur*, but, nevertheless, at the end of the case the judge must ask himself whether the legal burden is discharged. If the matter is left evenly in the balance, the plaintiff fails. But in public nuisance, as in trespass, the legal burden shifts to the defendant, and it is not sufficient for him to leave the matter in doubt. He must plead and prove a sufficient justification or excuse.

(5) *Justification or excuse.* The defendants seek to justify themselves by saying that it was necessary for them to discharge the oil because their ship was in danger. She had been driven by rough seas on to the revetment wall, and it was necessary to discharge the oil in order to get her off. If she had not done so, lives might have been lost. This is, no doubt, true at that stage in the story, but the question is, how came she to get upon the wall? If it was her own fault, then her justification fails, because no one can avail himself of a necessity produced by his own default. Where does the legal burden rest in this respect? Must the Southport Corporation prove that the ship was at fault in getting on to the wall, or must the ship prove that she herself was not at fault? In my opinion the burden is on the ship. She does not justify herself in law by necessity alone, but only by unavoidable necessity, and the burden is on her to show it was unavoidable.

Public nuisance is, in this respect, like unto a trespass, as to which it was said by the Court of King's Bench as long ago as 1616 in *Weaver v. Ward*, that no man shall be excused 'except it may be judged utterly without his fault.'

Those were, it is true, cases in trespass; but the same principle applies to cases of public nuisance. That is shown by *Tarry v. Ashton*, where a lamp which projected over the Strand fell on to a passer-by. This was described by Lord

Wright as private action for a public nuisance: see *Sedleigh-Denfield v. O'Callaghan.*

In fact the Court of Appeal's decision in favour of the claimant was reversed by the House of Lords. They upheld the trial judge's decision in favour of the defendants. Nevertheless there is still a 'forms of action' mentality that could be said to have attached to the House of Lords' approach. After Denning LJ's judgment the claimant tried to add a further cause of action to the four already pleaded; they wanted to argue in the House of Lords that, in putting to sea an unseaworthy ship, Esso was in breach of a direct (non-delegable) duty owed directly to the claimant.

Esso Petroleum Co Ltd v Southport Corporation [1956] AC 218
House of Lords

Lord Radcliffe: My Lords, I think that this case ought to be decided in accordance with the pleadings. If it is, I am of opinion, as was the trial judge, that the respondents failed to establish any claim to relief that was valid in law. If it is not, we might do better justice to the respondents – I cannot tell, since the evidence is incomplete – but I am certain that we should do worse justice to the appellants, since in my view they were entitled to conduct the case and confine their evidence in reliance upon the further and better particulars of the statement of claim which had been delivered by the respondents. It seems to me that it is the purpose of such particulars that they should help to define the issues and to indicate to the party who asks for them how much of the range of his possible evidence will be relevant and how much irrelevant to those issues. Proper use of them shortens the hearing and reduces costs. But if an appellate court is to treat reliance upon them as pedantry or mere formalism, I do not see what part they have to play in our trial system.

Lord Radcliffe seems to be saying that even though the claimant might in theory have had a 'right' to succeed (on the non-delegable duty point) he could not in practice succeed because he did not plead this cause of action at the outset. He had, one might say, not chosen the right 'form' of action.

Of course a 'form of action' is equivalent to a 'remedy' only in that they both can be described as actions. Modern remedies are more flexible. Nevertheless they can still act as the starting point for legal reasoning.

***Mercedes Benz AG v Leiduck* [1996] 1 AC 284 Privy Council**

Lord Nicholls (dissenting): ... Two preliminary points are to be noted. First, practising lawyers tend to think in terms of established categories of causes of action, such as those in contract or tort or trust or arising under statute. They do not always appreciate that the range of causes of action already extends very widely, into areas where identification of the underlying 'right' may be elusive. For instance, a writ may properly be issued containing nothing materially more than a claim for an injunction to restrain a defendant from continuing proceedings abroad on the ground that this would be unconscionable: see *British Airways Board v Laker Airways Ltd* [1985] AC 58, 81, 95; [1984] QB 142, 147. In such a case, the underlying right, if sought to be identified, can only be defined along the lines that a party has a right not to be sued abroad when that would be unconscionable. This formulation exemplifies the circular nature of the discussion. Second, originating process is not always concerned with the determination of an underlying dispute between the parties. For instance, a plaintiff may bring an action for discovery against a person, in respect of whom he has otherwise no cause of action, in aid of other proceedings not yet commenced: see *Norwich Pharmacal Co v Customs and Excise Commissioners* [1974] AC 133. In such a case the only relief sought is of an interim character in the sense that it is in aid of other proceedings.

A right to obtain an interlocutory injunction in aid of the substantive relief sought in an action is not normally regarded as a cause of action. This is because ordinarily proceedings bring a substantive dispute before the court. Attention is therefore focused on the cause of action involved in the substantive dispute the court is being asked to resolve. The claim to interim protective relief is ancillary to the underlying cause of action, and in that respect it has no independent existence of its own.

What this observation indicates is that it is not always easy to distinguish between 'right' and 'remedy'. And one might also note that the remedy being referred to by Lord Nicholls is an injunction; this is an equitable remedy and it thus attracts its own equitable rules.

3.6 EQUITABLE REMEDIES

In other words a remedies approach was equally to be found in the old Court of Chancery and thus equitable remedies like injunction, specific performance and account can still be an important starting point for judging.

***Attorney-General v Blake* [2001] 1 AC 268 House of Lords**

Lord Nicholls: ... Courts of equity went further than the common law courts. In some cases equity required the wrongdoer to yield up all his gains. In respect of certain wrongs which originally or ordinarily were the subject of proceedings in the Court of Chancery, the standard remedies were injunction and, incidental thereto, an account of profits. These wrongs included passing off, infringement of trade marks, copyrights and patents, and breach of confidence. Some of these subjects are now embodied in statutory codes. An injunction restrained the continuance of the wrong, and the wrongdoer was required to account for the profits or benefits he had obtained from breaches or infringements which had already occurred. The court always had a discretion regarding the grant of the remedy of an account of profits, and this remains the position. Further, the circumstances in which an account of profits is available under the statutes vary. For instance, an account of profits may not be ordered against a defendant in a patent infringement action who proves that at the date of the infringement he was not aware, and had no reasonable grounds for supposing, that the patent existed: Patents Act 1977, section 62(1).

The old common law courts could, with one exception (repossession of land), only grant monetary remedies (debt and damages). It was the old Court of Chancery that developed a range of non-monetary remedies: injunction, specific performance, rescission and rectification being the most notable. Account of profits is, however, an important monetary claim in equity; and this remedy used to be described as an equitable debt action.

***London, Chatham & Dover Railway Co v South Eastern Railway Co* [1892] 1 Ch 120 Court of Appeal**

Lindley LJ: ... Before the Judicature Acts a suit for an account could be maintained in equity in the following cases: – (1) Where the plaintiff had a legal right to have money payable to him ascertained and paid, but which right, owing to defective legal machinery, he could not practically enforce at law. Suits for an account between principal and agent, and between partners, are familiar instances of this class of case. (2) Where the plaintiff would have had a legal right to have money ascertained and paid to him by the defendant, if the defendant had not wrongfully prevented such right from accruing to the plaintiff. In such a case a court of law could only give unliquidated damages for the defendant's wrongful act; and there was often no machinery for satisfactorily ascertaining what would have been due and payable if the defendant had acted properly. In such a case, however, a Court of Equity decreed an account, ascertained what would have been payable if the defendant had acted as he ought to have done and ordered him to pay the amount: *M'Intosh v Great Western Railway Company* ((1865) 4 Giff 683), is the leading authority in this class of case. (3) Where the plaintiff had no legal but only equitable rights against the defendant, and where an account was necessary to give effect to those equitable rights. Ordinary suits by *cestuis que trust* against their trustees and suits for equitable waste fell within this class. (4) Combination of the above cases.

Account seems to be a useful remedy for preventing a person from profiting from the breach of an equitable and, sometimes, a common law obligation. Another such remedy is tracing.

Boscawen v Bajwa [1995] 4 All ER 769 Court of Appeal

Millett LJ: ... Equity lawyers habitually use the expressions 'the tracing claim' and 'the tracing remedy' to describe the proprietary claim and the proprietary remedy which equity makes available to the beneficial owner who seeks to recover his property in specie from those into whose hands it has come. Tracing properly so-called, however, is neither a claim nor a remedy but a process. Moreover, it is not confined to the case where the plaintiff seeks a proprietary remedy; it is equally necessary where he seeks a personal remedy against the knowing recipient or knowing assistant. It is the process by which the plaintiff traces what has happened to his property, identifies the persons who have handled or received it, and justifies his claim that the money which they handled or received (and if necessary which they still retain) can properly be regarded as representing his property. He needs to do this because his claim is based on the retention by him of a beneficial interest in the property which the defendant handled or received. Unless he can prove this, he cannot (in the traditional language of equity) raise an equity against the defendant or (in the modern language of restitution) show that the defendant's unjust enrichment was at his expense.

In such a case, the defendant will either challenge the plaintiff's claim that the property in question represents his property (ie he will challenge the validity of the tracing exercise), or he will raise a priority dispute (eg by claiming to be a bona fide purchaser without notice). If all else fails, he will raise the defence of innocent change of position. This was not a defence which was recognised in England before 1991, but it was widely accepted throughout the common law world. In *Lipkin Gorman (a firm) v Karpnale Ltd* [1991] 2 AC 548 the House of Lords acknowledged it to be part of English law also. The introduction of this defence not only provides the court with a means of doing justice in future, but allows a re-examination of many decisions of the past in which the absence of the defence may have led judges to distort basic principles in order to avoid injustice to the defendant.

If the plaintiff succeeds in tracing his property, whether in its original or in some changed form, into the hands of the defendant and overcomes any defences which are put forward on the defendant's behalf, he is entitled to a remedy. The remedy will be fashioned to the circumstances. The plaintiff will generally be entitled to a personal remedy; if he seeks a proprietary remedy he must usually prove that the property to which he lays claim is still in the ownership of the defendant. If he succeeds in doing this, the court will treat the

> defendant as holding the property on a constructive trust for the plaintiff and will order the defendant to transfer it *in specie* to the plaintiff. But this is only one of the proprietary remedies which is available to a court of equity. If the plaintiff's money has been applied by the defendant, for example, not in the acquisition of a landed property but in its improvement, then the court may treat the land as charged with the payment to the plaintiff of a sum representing the amount by which the value of the defendant's land has been enhanced by the use of the plaintiff's money. And if the plaintiff's money has been used to discharge a mortgage on the defendant's land, then the court may achieve a similar result by treating the land as subject to a charge by way of subrogation in favour of the plaintiff.

It would appear that tracing is not strictly a 'remedy' but a process. Nevertheless it acts as a kind of remedial focal point for deciding a case. It bears a certain similarity to the old Roman *actio in rem*. The owner, in effect, brings a claim against the thing itself based upon his 'ownership' of the *res*. In the remedies model this idea of suing people and suing things is fundamental; the first type of claim belongs, in private law, to the category of the law of obligations (*actiones in personam*) while actions against things (*actiones in rem*) belong in the law of property.

3.7 REMEDIES AND REASONING

How, then, does the remedies model of judging and reasoning function? It is really a question of where one starts. The rights model approaches judging from the position of a formalised, abstract and coherent (supposedly) system of pre-ordained rights expressed as 'axiomatic' principles (see 3.1). Do the facts reveal that the claimant has a right to the particular remedy claimed? A remedies approach, in contrast, starts out from the remedy itself: does the claimant justly deserve a remedy on these facts? This difference of approach can result in a different form of reasoning. A rights approach is strictly formal; one looks only at the abstract system of rights and views the facts in relation to this system. The ideal method is deductive in that the right can hopefully be expressed as a normative 'axiom' and applied to the facts through the employment of the syllogism – although where a word or expression is ambiguous the judge may have to adopt an interpretative (hermeneutical) approach in order to determine if the claimant actually has a right. A remedies approach, in contrast, may well adopt different kinds of reasoning models; it may combine the remedies approach with the interest model (see 3.4) or with the policy model (see 3.3) in order to decide if the claimant should succeed (see eg

Burris v Azadani [1995] 1 WLR 1372: see 3.4). Sometimes these different forms of reasoning can be seen to be employed in a single judgment.

> ***Co-operative Insurance Society Ltd v Argyll Stores Ltd* [1998] AC 1**
> **House of Lords**
>
> **Lord Hoffmann**: ... It is true that the defendant has, by his own breach of contract, put himself in such an unfortunate position. But the purpose of the law of contract is not to punish wrongdoing but to satisfy the expectations of the party entitled to performance. A remedy which enables him to secure, in money terms, more than the performance due to him is unjust. From a wider perspective, it cannot be in the public interest for the courts to require someone to carry on business at a loss if there is any plausible alternative by which the other party can be given compensation. It is not only a waste of resources but yokes the parties together in a continuing hostile relationship. The order for specific performance prolongs the battle. If the defendant is ordered to run a business, its conduct becomes the subject of a flow of complaints, solicitors' letters and affidavits. This is wasteful for both parties and the legal system. An award of damages, on the other hand, brings the litigation to an end. The defendant pays damages, the forensic link between them is severed, they go their separate ways and the wounds of conflict can heal.

Another characteristic of the remedies model is the emphasis on the facts together with the use of analogical reasoning. The old forms of action approach required one to match the facts of one's dispute with the model factual situations associated with each writ; if the facts of the dispute 'fitted' with the factual model of a writ the claimant could proceed to have his claim litigated. This kind of approach can still be in evidence today, as Denning LJ's judgment in *Esso v Southport Corporation* (see 3.5) indicates. Often this approach is expressed in terms of analogical reasoning.

> ***Goodwill v British Pregnancy Advisory Service* [1996] 1 WLR 1397**
> **Court of Appeal**
>
> **Peter Gibson LJ**: ... Miss Booth also relied on *White v Jones* [1995] 2 AC 207 as providing an example of an analogous situation in which a duty of care has been recognised. In that case a solicitor who was instructed to prepare a will but delayed in carrying out his instructions was held to owe a duty of care to the intended beneficiaries. She submitted that a woman who had a sexual relationship with Mr MacKinlay is in an analogous position to the intended beneficiaries under the will, because just as the solicitor was employed to confer a benefit (in the form of bequests) on a particular class of people (the beneficiaries), so the doctor is employed to confer a benefit (not getting pregnant) on a particular class

of people (women who have sexual relationships with Mr MacKinlay). I admire the ingenuity of the suggested analogy, but I have to say that I am wholly unpersuaded that the analogy is real.

Another reason that is sometimes used to justify the granting of a remedy in situations where the claimant's entitlement might appear weak (if one were one to adopt a 'rights' approach) is 'practical justice'.

Attorney-General v Blake **[2001] 1 AC 268 House of Lords**

Lord Steyn: ... Secondly, I bear in mind that the enduring strength of the common law is that it has been developed on a case-by-case basis by judges for whom the attainment of practical justice was a major objective of their work. It is still one of the major moulding forces of judicial decision-making. These observations are almost banal: the public would be astonished if it was thought that judges did not conceive it as their prime duty to do practical justice whenever possible. A recent example of this process at work is *White v Jones* [1995] 2 AC 207 where by a majority the House of Lords held that a solicitor who caused loss to a third party by negligence in the preparation of a will is liable in damages. Subordinating conceptual difficulties to the needs of practical justice a majority, and notably Lord Goff of Chieveley, at pp. 259G-260H, upheld the claim. For my part practical justice strongly militates in favour of granting an order for disgorgement of profits against Blake.

One might note Lord Steyn's expression about subordinating 'conceptual difficulties'. This perhaps brings out the contrast between the rights model (conceptual) and the remedies model (practical). Remedies are there as much to answer practical problems as to provide protection against invasions of rights.

3.8 REFLECTIONS ON THE OFFICIAL PORTRAIT

Six different 'official' models of reasoning have been identified so far. They have been labelled 'official' because they have been identified largely from the approaches, and the words, of the judges themselves. However, these different models should not be seen as being completely discrete; legal reasoning may often involve the combination of more than one model. Sometimes the same judge will employ different models in different cases. Moreover these models do not, by any means, explain in themselves the full complexities of legal reasoning. They should be seen as starting points, or points of emphasis, that encourage reasoning to go in a particular direction. Often the 'law' and its analysis do not point in one direction.

> ***Hunter v Canary Wharf Ltd* [1997] AC 655 House of Lords**
>
> **Lord Cooke** (dissenting in part): ... In logic more than one answer can be given. Logically it is possible to say that the right to sue for interference with the amenities of a home should be confined to those with proprietary interests and licensees with exclusive possession. No less logically the right can be accorded to all who live in the home. Which test should be adopted, that is to say which should be the governing principle, is a question of the policy of the law. It is a question not capable of being answered by analysis alone. All that analysis can do is expose the alternatives.

As Lord Cooke notes, logic depends on the premise adopted and thus starting out from a right might lead in one direction while focusing on a remedy and practical justice might well lead in another direction. Even within the interpretation model the premise in play can be vital.

> ***Whittaker v Campbell* [1984] QB 318 Queen's Bench Division**
>
> **Robert Goff LJ**: ... We are concerned in the present case with the construction of certain words, viz., 'without having the consent of the owner', in their context in a particular subsection of a criminal statute. However, the concept of consent is relevant in many branches of the law, including not only certain crimes but also the law of contract and the law of property. There is, we believe, danger in assuming that the law adopts a uniform definition of the word 'consent' in all its branches ...

Defining a term such as 'consent' or 'possession' might well depend upon the category of law in issue. There is no single definition, once asserted, that will apply across the whole of the law (although see *Fisher v Bell* [1961] 1 QB 394). Logic itself may be abandoned if the policy consideration proves stronger.

> ***Parry v Cleaver* [1970] AC 1 House of Lords**
>
> **Lord Reid**: ... It would be revolting to the ordinary man's sense of justice, and therefore contrary to public policy, that the sufferer should have his damages reduced so that he would gain nothing from the benevolence of his friends or relations or of the public at large, and that the only gainer would be the wrongdoer.

The judges are conscious that legal reasoning cannot be just a matter of deduction from some abstract model. The impact of their decisions on the public is to be considered.

Academic lawyers, in contrast, do not always share the same view of legal reasoning and argumentation as the judges. Academics like to propound and defend theories. Thus, as we have seen, rights theorists may well find themselves opposed to theorists who are more functionalist in their views and who, therefore, may be more attracted to the policy and (or) to the remedies model. As for the judges themselves, they are, perhaps, more wary of theory.

Broome v Cassell & Co Ltd [1972] AC 1027 House of Lords

Lord Wilberforce (dissenting): ... English law does not work in an analytical fashion; ... That is why the terminology used is empirical and not scientific. And there is more than merely practical justification for this attitude. For particularly over the range of torts for which punitive damages may be given (trespass to person or property, false imprisonment and defamation being the commonest) there is much to be said before one can safely assert that the true or basic principle of the law of damages in tort is compensation, or, if it is, what the compensation is for (if one says that a plaintiff is given compensation because he has been injured, one is really denying the word its true meaning) or, if there is compensation, whether there is not in all cases, or at least in some, of which defamation may be an example, also a delictual element which contemplates some penalty for the defendant. It cannot lightly be taken for granted, even as a matter of theory, that the purpose of the law of tort is compensation, still less that it ought to be, an issue of large social import, or that there is something inappropriate or illogical or anomalous (a question-begging word) in including a punitive element in civil damages, or, conversely, that the criminal law, rather than the civil law, is in these cases the better instrument for conveying social disapproval, or for redressing a wrong to the social fabric, or that damages in any case can be broken down into the two separate elements. As a matter of practice English law has not committed itself to any of these theories: it may have been wiser than it knew.

... Take a common case: a man is assaulted, or his land is trespassed upon, with accompanying circumstances of insolence or contumely. He decides to bring an action for damages, he need not further specify the claim. Is he suing for compensation, for injury to his feelings, to teach his opponent a lesson, to vindicate his rights, or 'the strength of the law,' or for a mixture of these things? Most men would not ask themselves such questions, many men could not answer them. If they could answer them, they might give different answers. The reaction to a libel may be anything from 'how outrageous' to 'he has delivered himself into my hands.' The fact is that the plaintiff sues for damages, inviting the court to take all the facts into consideration, and, if he wins, he may ascribe his victory to all or any of the ingredients.

Lord Wilberforce was primarily talking about the aims of the law of tort, but the essence of what he was saying is summed up by his opening words in the above extract. As we shall see, the judges are not committed to a single theory or model and nor do they always reason in an analytical fashion. And it is a senior judge who has asserted this point; that is to say it forms part of the 'official portrait' of judging and reasoning.

FURTHER READING AND QUESTIONS

1. There is a huge literature on rights and this can be accessed via many textbooks on jurisprudence. However Hohfeld (1919) remains the classic analytical theory. A key work on remedies was Lawson (1980), which is a bit dated now and can usefully be supplemented by Zakrzewski (2005). For a brief overview of remedies see Samuel (2013, pp 50–71). The classic work on the notion of an interest remains Ost (1990) (in French), but this is not available in translation.
2. If one applies a traditional Roman law analysis, substantive rights arise from the law of persons and the law of things while remedies belong to the law of actions. How should one describe the relationship between rights and remedies in English law? Do remedies follow the right or do rights follow the availability of remedies? Might remedies attract their own particular rules that could indirectly modify substantive law rights?
3. Is it too simplistic to reduce legal reasoning to one of the six models set out in this chapter and the previous one? Does not legal reasoning often involve the intermixing of more than one model?
4. 'English law does not work in an analytical fashion' (Lord Wilberforce). Discuss.

4. The 'unofficial portrait'

The models of reasoning that have been considered so far can be said to make up an 'official portrait' of legal reasoning. These models are not inaccurate or misleading as such (hopefully quite the opposite), but they reveal only part of what constitutes legal reasoning. They are largely formalist models. In addition to these models there is what might be called an 'unofficial portrait' (this unofficial portrait metaphor is again taken from Mitchel Lasser, (2004)).

4.1 REALIST VISION

Part of this unofficial portrait can be described as 'realist' in its approach. That is to say it looks at the reality of legal reasoning – at what a sociologist might have to say about it. The major source of this school of thought was the American Realist movement, which was active in the first half of the 20th century, although its effects have continued up until the present day ('we are all Realists now' said William Twining).

Jerome Frank, *Law and the Modern Mind*, Stevens & Sons, 1949, pp x–xi

If one accepts as correct the conventional description of how courts reach their decisions, then a decision of any lawsuit results from the application of a legal rule or rules to the facts of the suit. That sounds rather simple, and apparently renders it fairly easy to prophesy the decision, even of a case not yet commenced or tried, especially when, as often happens, the applicable rule is definite and precise (for instance, the rule about driving on the right side of the road). But, particularly when pivotal testimony at the trial is oral and conflicting, as it is in most lawsuits, the trial court's 'finding' of the facts involves a multitude of elusive factors: First, the trial judge in a non-jury trial or the jury in a jury trial must learn about the facts from the witnesses; and witnesses, being humanly fallible, frequently make mistakes in observation of what they saw and heard, or in their recollections of what they observed, or in their court-room reports of those recollections. Second, the trial judges or juries, also human, may have prejudices – often unconscious, unknown even to themselves – for or against some of the witnesses, or the parties to the suit, or the lawyers.

Those prejudices, when they are racial, religious, political, or economic, may sometimes be surmised by others. But there are some hidden, unconscious biases of trial judges or jurors – such as, for example, plus or minus reactions to women, or unmarried women, or red-haired women, or brunettes, or men with deep voices or high-pitched voices, or fidgety men, or men who wear thick eyeglasses, or those who have pronounced gestures or nervous ticks – biases of which no one can be aware. Concealed and highly idiosyncratic, such biases – peculiar to each individual judge or juror – cannot be formulated as uniformities or squeezed into regularized 'behaviour patterns'. In that respect, neither judges nor jurors are standardized.

The chief obstacle to prophesying a trial court decision is, then, the inability, thanks to these inscrutable factors, to foresee what a particular trial judge or jury will believe to be the facts. …

Is legal reasoning a matter of political bias?

JAG Griffith, *The Politics of the Judiciary*, Fontana, 3rd ed, 1985, pp 225–226

My thesis is that judges in the United Kingdom cannot be politically neutral because they are placed in positions where they are required to make political choices …; that their interpretation … is determined by the kind of people they are and the position they hold in our society; that this position is a part of established authority and so is necessarily conservative and illiberal. From all this flows … judicial attitudes such as tenderness towards private property and dislike of trade unions, strong adherence to the maintenance of order, distaste for minority opinions, demonstrations and protests, indifference to the promotion of better race relations, support of government secrecy, concern for the preservation of the moral and social behaviour to which it is accustomed, and the rest …

One should not be surprised that judicial decision making will reflect the social background, gender and political beliefs of the judiciary. Thus it must be of some concern that the great majority of England's senior judges are white, male, public school and Oxbridge (*The Guardian*, 14 July 2015, 39). One can only respond by emphasising the importance of gender balance and more diversity in social background. This will not of course solve the question about social bias.

Thus some cases do indeed force judges to show their political and social leanings.

R v Secretary of State for Work and Pensions [2015] UKSC 16 Supreme Court

Lord Reed: … **66.** The third aim, of imposing a reasonable limit upon the total amount which a household can receive in welfare benefits, is in my opinion equally legitimate. It is again an aspect of securing the economic well-being of the country: it is one of the means of achieving that objective. It also however has a broader aspect, namely to reflect a political view as to the nature of a fair and healthy society. As Ministers explained to Parliament, this objective responds in particular to a public perception that the benefits system has been excessively generous to some recipients: a perception which is related to the stigmatisation in the media of non-working households receiving high levels of benefit. The maintenance of public confidence in the welfare system, so that recipients are not stigmatised or resented, is undeniably a legitimate aim. In the language used by the European court in *Hoogendijk* and other cases, the benefit system is the means by which society expresses solidarity with its most vulnerable members. That being so, it is in principle legitimate to reform the system when necessary to respond to a threat to that solidarity. …

Lady Hale (dissenting): … **180.** The prejudicial effect of the cap is obvious and stark. It breaks the link between benefit and need. Claimants affected by the cap will, by definition, not receive the sums of money which the state deems necessary for them adequately to house, feed, clothe and warm themselves and their children. Furthermore, the greater the need, the greater the adverse effect. The more children there are in a family, the less each of them will have to live on. Ms SG, for example, will receive no more benefit if her 12 year old son rejoins the family, even though a court (either here or in Belgium) has decided that it is in his best interests to do so. This prejudicial effect has a disproportionate impact upon lone parents, the great majority of whom are women, and is also said to have such an impact upon victims of domestic violence, most of whom are also women. …

229. Viewed in the light of the primary consideration of the best interests of the children affected, therefore, the indirect discrimination against women inherent in the way in which the benefit cap has been implemented cannot be seen as a proportionate means of achieving a legitimate aim. Families in work are already better off than those on benefits and so the cap is not necessary in order to achieve fairness between them; saving money cannot be achieved by unjustified discrimination; but the major aim, of incentivising work and changing the benefits culture, has little force in the context of lone parents, whatever the age of their children. Depriving them of the basic means of subsistence cannot be a proportionate means of achieving it. …

The political outlooks of these two judges are, evidently, very different. One might add that the gender difference is probably of equal importance, although Lady Hale was not the only dissenting judge in this case.

What if all five judges had been women? Would the result of the case have been different?

Zoe Williams, 'Porn judges have set a new benchmark', *The Guardian*, 18 March 2015, p 37

Judges are notorious for being stuck in the past: for not knowing who the Beatles are, for needing text messages – indeed the existence of mobile phones – explained to them. ...

The problem with this kind of detachment, this ability to remain resolutely two or three decades behind everyone else, has other effects, which are visible throughout the profession: a failure to process diversity, to overcome their own bigotry.

Only 15.5% of high court judges are women, and 4.5% are from an ethnic background; only 10.5% on the court of appeal are women, and there are none with an ethnic background. ...

These statistics cannot be disputed (see *The Guardian*, 14 July 2015, 39), but is it true to say that all of the judges in the appeal courts are ignorant of texting and mobile telephones? One could argue that this was the case a couple of decades ago (although of course texting and mobiles were in their infancy) and no doubt there are still judges who conform to the pattern outlined by Zoe Williams. However the white, male and Oxbridge bias continues to dominate the higher judiciary.

Amelia Gentleman, 'Guess who's not coming to dinner', *The Guardian*, 30 April 2015, 35, p 37

There is growing hostility among women in the legal profession towards a club that welcomes so many male QCs and judges, but excludes women. In 2011, Baroness Hale, Britain's most senior female judge, the first and only woman among 12 supreme court judges – several of whom are Garrick Club members – told a law diversity forum: 'I regard it as quite shocking that so many of my colleagues belong to the Garrick Club, but they don't see what all the fuss is about'. Judges, she said, 'should be committed to the principle of equality for all'.

Conflicts of opinion between members of the judiciary reveal fundamental differences between them with respect to social and economic outlook.

***Tomlinson v Congleton BC* [2004] 1 AC 46 House of Lords**

Lord Hoffmann: ... **46.** ... I find it difficult to express with appropriate moderation my disagreement with the proposition of Sedley LJ [2003] 2 WLR 1120, 1135, para 45, that it is 'only where the risk is so obvious that the occupier can safely assume that nobody will take it that there will be no liability'. ...

These conflicts of outlook are by no means recent and are often linked to differences of economic outlook.

> ***Wildtree Hotels Ltd v Harrow LBC* [2001] 2 AC 1 House of Lords**
>
> **Lord Hoffmann**: ... The construction of the railways, which gave rise to most of the 19th century cases on injurious affection, involved massive changes in the urban and rural landscape of the United Kingdom and the disruption of the lives and businesses of very large numbers of people. It is not surprising that strong views were held about the respective claims of the winners and losers in this revolution and the judicial decisions often reveal the opinions of individual judges on questions of economic and social policy. Some were in favour of full compensation for all whose property had been adversely affected by the railway and others thought that the public interest required that liability should be kept within narrow bounds. ...
>
> In modern economic terms, Bramwell B thought that the railways should not create externalities; that is, costs involuntarily borne by other people which were not taken into account in assessing the profitability of the enterprise. The contrary view is exemplified by Erle CJ in *Ricket v Metropolitan Railway Co* (1865) 5 B & S 149, 163, 169 ... Judges who took this view tended to rely upon a floodgates argument: unless the right to compensation was rigidly confined, everyone whose economic interests had been damaged by the construction of the railways would be entitled to compensation. Post houses and coaching inns were favourite examples.
>
> My Lords, I mention these ancient controversies not only because they still have some resonance today but also because they are an aid to the understanding of the old cases to which your Lordships were referred in the course of the argument. The 19th century authorities on this subject do not display a steady development of the law but the shifting ascendancies of one view or the other. ...

Can it thus be said that the judges arrive at their decisions on the basis of their own political, social and (or) economic beliefs? It would be naïve to think that such beliefs have no influence. One might dream of a completely neutral and computer-like application of rules or rights, but such dreams are unrealistic if only because, as we shall see, it is questionable whether legal knowledge does consist only of rules.

4.2 FACTS AND REASONING

If one returns to Jerome Frank, he was one of the leading American Realists, who was often described as a 'fact sceptic'. As we shall see, how facts are categorised can be crucial; 'before the law can be applied the facts must be categorised but before the facts can be categorised the law must be applied' (to quote an old examination question). This point was echoed by another leading American Realist.

> **K Llewellyn, *The Bramble Bush*, Oceana, 1951, p 48**
>
> What are *the* facts? The plaintiff's name is Atkinson and the defendant's Walpole. The defendant, despite his name, is an Italian by extraction, but the plaintiff's ancestors came over with the Pilgrims. The defendant has a schnautzer-dog named Walter, red hair, and $30,000 worth of life insurance. All these are facts. The case, however, does not deal with life assurance. It is about an auto accident. The defendant's auto was a Buick painted pale magenta. He is married. His wife was in the back seat, an irritable somewhat faded blonde. She was attempting backseat driving when the accident occurred. He had turned around to make objection. In the process the car swerved and hit the plaintiff. The sun was shining; there was a rather lovely dappled sky low to the West. The time was late October on a Tuesday. The road was smooth, concrete. It had been put in by the McCarthy Road Work Company. How many of these facts are, as we say, legally relevant? Is it relevant that the road was in the country or in the city; that it was concrete or tarmac or of dirt; that it was a private or a public way? Is it relevant that the defendant was driving a Buick, or a motor car, or a vehicle? Is it important that he looked around as the car swerved? Is it crucial? Would it have been the same if he had been drunk, or had swerved for fun, to see how close he could run by the plaintiff, but had missed his guess?

As Llewellyn said, all these are facts but not all of them are relevant to the auto accident case. It is thus a question of level.

> **Stephen Waddams, *Dimensions of Private Law: Categories and Concepts in Anglo-American Legal Reasoning*, Cambridge University Press, 2003, p 14**
>
> Another obstacle to conceptual organization has been the complexity of the relation between facts and law. The facts of a case are defined in relation to legal principles, but the principles themselves are formulated in relation to facts, real or hypothetical. Facts may be stated at countless levels of particularity, and legal issues and legal rules may be formulated at countless levels of generality. No map or scheme could possibly classify all imaginable facts, for there is no limit whatever to the number of facts that may be postulated of a sequence of human events. The selection of legally relevant facts is a matter not of empirical investigation but of judgment, and not wholly separable from the formulation of the applicable legal rule.

How facts are envisaged is thus vital in the process of judging. Yet it is not just a question of the level of generality. There is what might be called an image or representation factor; the way a person – claimant or defendant – is represented can be fundamental to the decision in a case.

> ***Miller v Jackson* [1977] QB 966 Court of Appeal**
>
> **Lord Denning MR**: In summer time village cricket is the delight of everyone. Nearly every village has its own cricket field where the young men play and the old men watch. In the village of Lintz in County Durham they have their own ground, where they have played these last 70 years … Yet now after these 70 years a judge of the High Court has ordered that they must not play there any more. He has issued an injunction to stop them. He has done it at the instance of a newcomer who is no lover of cricket. This newcomer has built, or has had built for him, a house on the edge of the cricket ground which four years ago was a field where cattle grazed. The animals did not mind the cricket. But now this adjoining field has been turned into a housing estate … Now he complains that, when a batsman hits a six, the ball has been known to land in his garden or on or near his house. His wife has got so upset about it that they always go out at weekends. They do not go into the garden when cricket is being played. …
>
> **Cumming-Bruce LJ**: … As it turns out, the female plaintiff has developed a somewhat obsessive attitude to the proximity of the cricket field and the cricketers who visit her to seek to recover their cricket balls. The evidence discloses a hostility which goes beyond what is reasonable, although as the learned judge found she is reasonable in her fear that if the family use the garden while a match is in progress they will run the risk of serious injury … It is reasonable to decide that during matches the family must keep out of the garden. …

In this case two of the judges have constructed an image of the female plaintiff as being unreasonable. The third judge was actually far more sympathetic and felt that she was not being unreasonable to fear cricket balls coming into her garden. Not surprisingly he was more in favour of granting the injunction. One might ask if the two judges above are displaying a somewhat sexist attitude and, if so, whether this sexism affected their decision. Moreover one might ask if sexism is the only bias? Could the private education of the judge colour his judgment?

> ***Wainwright v Home Office* [2004] 2 AC 406 House of Lords**
>
> **Lord Scott**: … **62.** … The issue of importance in the present case is whether the infliction of humiliation and distress by conduct calculated to humiliate and cause distress, is without more, tortious at common law. I am in full agreement with the reasons that have been given by Lord Hoffmann for concluding that it is not. Nor, in my opinion, should it be. Some institutions, schools, university colleges, regiments and the like (often bad ones) have initiation ceremonies and rites which newcomers are expected to undergo. Ritual humiliation is often a part of

this. The authorities in charge of these institutions usually object to these practices and seek to put an end to any excesses. But why, absent any of the traditional nominate torts such as assault, battery, negligent causing of harm etc, should the law of tort intrude? If a shop assistant or a bouncer or barman at a club is publicly offensive to a customer, the customer may well be humiliated and distressed. But that is no sufficient reason why the law of tort should be fashioned and developed with a view to providing compensation in money to the victim. ...

On the continent it is unlikely that judges would adopt this kind of reasoning, even in their reports written for other members of the court. When a public institution is in issue the question would be whether a public official had legal power, as provided in a specific legal text, to humiliate a citizen. 'Initiation ceremonies' would probably not enter into the argument. If there was no text empowering the official to humiliate, there would be liability in administrative law.

4.3 FACT RECONSTRUCTION AND REMEDIES

One might also see this reasoning in *Wainwright* as falling within the remedies model (above 3.5). The Law Lord did not consider a remedy should issue on these facts and thus held that they did not fall into one of the cause of action categories (cf *Esso v Southport Corporation*, above 3.5). A fact-construction approach was equally taken in a leading contract case where substantial damages for a new swimming pool were refused despite the claimant seemingly having a contractual 'right' to be put into the position he would have been in if the contract had been performed correctly (that is to say that the pool conformed to the contractual measurements, which it did not).

***Ruxley Electronics Ltd v Forsyth* [1996] 1 AC 344 House of Lords**

Lord Jauncey: ... I take the example suggested during argument by my noble and learned friend, Lord Bridge of Harwich. A man contracts for the building of a house and specifies that one of the lower courses of brick should be blue. The builder uses yellow brick instead. In all other respects the house conforms to the contractual specification. To replace the yellow bricks with blue would involve extensive demolition and reconstruction at a very large cost. It would clearly be unreasonable to award to the owner the cost of reconstructing because his loss was not the necessary cost of reconstruction of his house, which was entirely adequate for its design purpose, but merely the lack of aesthetic pleasure which he might have derived from the sight of blue bricks. Thus in the present appeal the respondent has acquired a perfectly serviceable swimming pool, albeit one lacking the specified depth. His loss is thus not the lack of a useable pool with consequent need to construct a new one. Indeed were he to receive the cost of building a new one and retain the existing one he would have recovered not compensation for loss but a very substantial gratuitous benefit, something which damages are not intended to provide.

The reasoning method is rather subtle in this case. In the Court of Appeal the majority held that the contractor, an exceptionally tall person, was entitled to damages equalling the cost of a new swimming pool to replace the one that did not conform to the contract specifications (it did not have a depth of seven foot six inches as required by the contract, only six foot nine inches). The Court of Appeal arrived at its decision on the basis of logic: (1) *pacta sunt servanda* (contracts must be kept); (2) this contract was breached; (3) a victim of a breach of contract is entitled to his expectation interest (ie to be put in the position he would have been in had the contract not been breached); (4) (conclusion) the victim is entitled to the cost of a new swimming pool (£21,560). The trial judge and the House of Lords avoided this logical conclusion by shifting the focus off the swimming pool as the source of the damage – it was a perfectly 'reasonable' pool said the trial judge even though it did not conform to the contract – and onto the mind of the claimant. His actual damage, they said, was his disappointment in not having the pool he wanted. This damage was worth only £2,500 damages and that was what the trial judge, ultimately supported by the House of Lords, awarded. Fitting facts into categories or classes can also arise in cases involving statutes.

4.4 INTERPRETATION AND SCHEMES OF INTELLIGIBILITY

Accordingly how one views facts is equally important in statutory (and other texts) interpretation problems.

Animals Act 1971 (c 22)

2. Liability for damage done by dangerous animals.

(1) Where any damage is caused by an animal which belongs to a dangerous species, any person who is a keeper of the animal is liable for the damage, except as otherwise provided by this Act.

(2) Where damage is caused by an animal which does not belong to a dangerous species, a keeper of the animal is liable for the damage, except as otherwise provided by this Act, if—

(a) the damage is of a kind which the animal, unless restrained, was likely to cause or which, if caused by the animal, was likely to be severe; and

(b) the likelihood of the damage or of its being severe was due to characteristics of the animal which are not normally found in animals of the same species or are not normally so found except at particular times or in particular circumstances; and

(c) those characteristics were known to that keeper or were at any time known to a person who at that time had charge of the animal as that keeper's servant or, where that keeper is the head of a household, were known to another keeper of the animal who is a member of that household and under the age of sixteen.

An animal panics and causes a serious road accident. Is the keeper of this animal to be strictly liable under section 2(2)?

Mirvahedy v Henley [2003] 2 AC 491 House of Lords

This was an action for damages brought by a car driver against the owner of a horse that had escaped from a field in a panic and collided with the claimant's car causing him severe personal injury. The trial judge found that the escape had not been due to any negligence on the part of the defendant and the sole question, therefore, was whether liability could be established under the Animals Act 1971 s 2(2). A majority of the House of Lords (Lords Nicholls, Hobhouse and Walker; Lords Slynn and Scott dissenting) held that there was liability under the section.

Lord Hobhouse: … **69.** Horses are not normally in a mindless state of panic nor do they normally ignore obstacles in their path. These characteristics are normally only found in horses in circumstances where they have been very seriously frightened. It is only in such circumstances that it becomes likely that, due to these characteristics, the horse will cause severe damage. This case clearly comes within the words of s.2(2)(b). There is no ambiguity either about the facts of this case or about the meaning of paragraph (b). …

Lord Scott (dissenting): … **130.** A clear answer to the question as to the proper construction of paragraph (b) cannot, in my opinion, be obtained from the actual language of the provision, nor from a perusal of Hansard, nor from examining the contents of the Law Commission Report of 1967 on which the 1971 Act was in part based. The answer depends upon identifying what Parliament appears to have been trying to achieve. It seems to me that Parliament was trying to draw a distinction between animals that in normal circumstances behaving normally are dangerous and those that in normal circumstances behaving normally are not. As to the former, they belong to a dangerous species and there was to be strict liability for damage; as to the latter they do not belong to a dangerous species and strict liability was to be limited to damage caused by the animal displaying abnormal characteristics that it was known by its keeper to possess. This seems to me to be a coherent policy. In respect of damage for which no strict liability was imposed, a remedy in negligence would always be available if the keeper of the animal had failed to exercise reasonable care to see that the animal did not cause damage. The keeper's knowledge of the circumstances in which and times at which the animal might be likely to become dangerous and cause damage would, of course, be highly relevant in determining the standard of care required to be observed by the keeper. A standard of care can, in appropriate circumstances, be placed so high as to require the person subject to it to become virtually an insurer against damage. …

The difference of opinion between the two judges extracted above is to be found in a difference of schemes of intelligibility (on which see 6.1). Lord Hobhouse adopted a structural scheme in which he matches the conceptual structure of the legislative section with a structured view of the facts; there is the notion of 'characteristics' related to the notion of 'not normally found'. This matches with panic (characteristic) and horse (not normally found) and so there is liability. Lord Scott adopts a very different scheme; he takes a functional approach and asks what the section was trying to do. The two different schemes of intelligibility employed by the judges resulted in different decisions.

Another scheme of intelligibility is hermeneutics (see further 6.2 and 6.6). This is based on the idea that a text or a work of art is a signifier and what needs to be discovered is what the signifier signifies. What does the text or painting mean?

Re Rowland [1963] Ch 1 Court of Appeal

Lord Denning MR (dissenting): … I decline … to ask myself: what do the words mean to a grammarian? I prefer to ask: What did Dr Rowland and his wife mean by the word 'coincide' in their wills? When they came to make their wills it is not difficult to piece together the thoughts that ran through their minds. The doctor might well say: 'We are going off for three years to these far off places and in case anything happens to either of us we ought to make our wills. If I die before you, I would like everything to go to you, but if you die before me, I should like it to go to my brother and his boy'. She might reply: 'Yes, but what if we both die together. After all, one of those little ships might run on the rocks or something and we might both be drowned; or we might both be killed in an aeroplane crash'. 'To meet that,' he would say, 'I will put in that if your death coincides with mine, it is to go to my brother and his boy just the same'. He would use the words 'coinciding with', not in the narrow meaning of 'simultaneous', but in the wider meaning of which they are equally capable, especially in this context, as denoting death on the same occasion by the same cause. It would not cross Dr Rowland's mind that anyone would think of such niceties as counsel for the first defendant has presented to us.

Russell LJ: … If the evidence was that the testator and his wife were below decks in their cabin and the vessel plunged abruptly to the bottom of the sea, the view might be taken that their deaths were, metaphysics apart, coincident in point of time. But we simply do not know what happened to them. Counsel for the appellants could not suggest, in the case of either spouse, whether the correct inference was death by drowning, trapped in the ship, or death by drowning, sucked down by the sinking ship after going overboard, or death by shark or similar fish, or by thirst, or by drowning after swimming about or floating for a greater or less period with or without a lifebelt. This makes it plain that there is no evidence at all that the deaths were coincident in point of time (in the natural sense of simultaneous) in the mind of the ordinary man.

The difference between the two judges in *Rowland* can be explained by reference to what can be called a holist and a nominalist approach. Lord Denning takes a holistic view of a ship sinking; it is a single event and thus the couple died at the same time. Russell LJ adopts a nominalistic view. He does not see the sinking as a single event, for that is just a name (*nomina*); he sees it as a series of individual details. The debate goes back to the medieval philosophers who asked questions like: do forests exist? The response from the nominalists was that only trees exist and 'forest' is simply a name. It exists only in the mind and not in reality. There is of course a fictional element to the reasoning here. Lord Denning resorts to creating a piece of theatre with a script written by him; the other judge seems more inclined to a *Jaws* vision of the event. Both judges are inventing scenarios.

4.5 REASONING THROUGH IMAGES

The case of *Re Rowland* indicated the role that pictures and images can assume in arriving at, or supporting, a decision. Lord Denning and Russell LJ presented differing images of what happened. A similar comment could be made about *Miller v Jackson*. This resort to images is sometimes described as non-symbolic knowledge; it is knowledge that does not use the symbols of written language or numbers but relies upon visual associations. However, in order to understand this distinction between the two kinds of knowledge, one needs to appreciate, first of all, the advantages and disadvantages that attach to symbolic knowledge.

Jean Delacour, *Le cerveau et l'esprit*, Presses Universitaires de France, 1995, pp 31, 33–34 (translation Geoffrey Samuel)

The cognitive sciences consider symbols in general (we will leave aside those of religious or artistic origin) as objects of simple structure, of weak dimension in the sense defined later. This characteristic is the effect of a more general property: any symbol is either an object entirely constructed from other objects of the same nature but more simple or an element of these constructions. These rules allow basic symbols to be become elements of a system. The typical examples are numbers and words. ...

Symbols are then a simplification of representations which facilitates their communication, their conservation in non-living memories and their treatment through logico-mathematics, executable by machines (conventional digital computers for example). It is difficult to communicate, conserve and to handle every bit of information contained in a perception, even something as banal as that of a book on a table. In contrast it is easy to communicate any linguistic description of an object, even in detail, and to translate it into a system of signs which will allow a computer to store it and to subject it to a range of operations. These advantages of the symbol come at a price that in the absence of a more rigorous language there is a loss of information, a loss of dimension. ...

Thus the symbolic spirit, as it manifests itself in contemporary industrial societies, has a tendency to reduce the dimension and complexity of objects. ...

This symbolic knowledge can be contrasted with non-symbolic knowledge.

Jean Delacour, *Le cerveau et l'esprit*, Presses Universitaires de France, 1995, pp 35–36 (translation Geoffrey Samuel)

1/ Are all mental representations symbolic? Are they equivalent to a linguistic expression, to a sentence? Against this thesis there is the observation that the content of most representations is made up not of symbols but of images, emotional states, schemes and prototypes which are often untranslatable into a linguistic expression. When a translation is possible it is accompanied by a considerable loss of information and dimension (see previous section). This last point, relatively little considered, seems to us to be of great importance both for the understanding of the functional significance of and the limits for the usage of symbolic representations. ...

If one returns to legal reasoning, the distinction between symbolic and non-symbolic knowledge does seem to find expression in the words of some judges.

***Hall v Lorimer* [1992] 1 WLR 939 Queen's Bench Division**

Mummery J: ... In order to decide whether a person carries on business on his own account it is necessary to consider many different aspects of that person's work activity. This is not a mechanical exercise of running through items on a check list to see whether they are present in, or absent from, a given situation. The object of the exercise is to paint a picture from the accumulation of detail. The overall effect can only be appreciated by standing back from the detailed picture which has been painted, by viewing it from a distance and by making an informed, considered, qualitative appreciation of the whole. It is a matter of evaluation of the overall effect of the detail, which is not necessarily the same as the sum total of the individual details. Not all details are of equal weight or importance in any given situation. The details may also vary in importance from one situation to another.

The use of metaphors is another example of image reasoning.

Spartan Steel & Alloys Ltd v Martin & Co (Contractors) Ltd [1973] 1 QB 27 Court of Appeal

Lord Denning MR: ... I do not like this doctrine of 'parasitic damages'. I do not like the very word 'parasite'. A 'parasite' is one who is a useless hanger-on sucking the substance out of others. 'Parasitic' is the adjective derived from it. It is a term of abuse. It is an opprobrious epithet. The phrase 'parasitic damages' conveys to my mind the idea of damages which ought not in justice to be awarded, but which somehow or other have been allowed to get through by hanging on to others. If such be the concept underlying the doctrine, then the sooner it is got rid of the better. ...

The employment of metaphors in legal reasoning – indeed in reasoning and argumentation in general – must never be underestimated. They have a central role in creating images in the mind.

Marie-Laure Mathieu, _Les représentations dans la pensée des juristes_, IRJS Éditions, 2014, p 44 (translation Geoffrey Samuel)

If analogy is happy to emphasise the similarity between two *objects*, metaphor highlights the similarity between two *relations between objects*. In other words analogy is limited to establishing *a* single relation (between whatever two objects) while metaphor brings into play *three*, which are situated at different levels: the two relations that they take as objects, and the relation of similarity that it establishes between these two relations between objects, and which is situated on another level.

If one returns to Lord Denning's parasite metaphor one can explain these three relations. There is (1) the relation between the remedy of damages and pure economic loss which attaches to some physical damage and (2) the relation between a parasite and the living creature to which it attaches. The third relation (3) is the supposed similarity between these two other relations. As Professor Mathieu goes on to show, metaphor is fundamental to legal thought: expressions such as '*vinculum iuris*' (legal chain used in the definition of an obligation), 'source' of law, 'pyramid' of norms (Hans Kelsen) and so on are so common that one often fails to see that they are metaphors. They can form the basis of models and theories in law as well as providing images in argumentation.

4.6 REASONING AND THE *PERSONA*

This use of metaphor and image has been particularly powerful with respect to legal personality.

> ***HL Bolton (Engineering) Co Ltd v TJ Graham & Sons Ltd* [1956] Ch 577 Court of Appeal**
>
> **Denning LJ**: ... A company may in many ways be likened to a human body. It has a brain and nerve centre which controls what it does. It also has hands which hold the tools and act in accordance with directions from the centre. Some of the people in the company are mere servants and agents who are nothing more than hands to do the work and cannot be said to represent the mind or will. Others are directors and managers who represent the directing mind and will of the company, and control what it does. The state of mind of these managers is the state of mind of the company and is treated by the law as such.

In the civil law world there was much debate during the 19th century as to whether corporate legal entities were a reality or just a legal fiction. However according to English law the company is a fictional creation.

> ***Tesco Supermarkets Ltd v Nattrass* [1972] AC 153 House of Lords**
>
> **Lord Reid**: ... I must start by considering the nature of the personality which by a fiction the law attributes to a corporation. A living person has a mind which can have knowledge or intention or be negligent and he has hands to carry out his intentions. A corporation has none of these: it must act through living persons, though not always one or the same person. Then the person who acts is not speaking or acting for the company. He is acting as the company and his mind which directs his acts is the mind of the company. There is no question of the company being vicariously liable. He is not acting as a servant, representative, agent or delegate. He is an embodiment of the company or, one could say, he hears and speaks through the persona of the company, within his appropriate sphere, and his mind is the mind of the company. If it is a guilty mind then that guilt is the guilt of the company. It must be a question of law whether, once the facts have been ascertained, a person in doing particular things is to be regarded as the company or merely as the company's servant or agent. In that case any liability of the company can only be a statutory or vicarious liability. ...

The problem which arose in *Tesco* concerned the defence in the Trade Descriptions Act of 'another person'. A mislabelling of the price of a product on a supermarket shelf prima facie is a crime but if the defendant (in this case a company) can show that the act of mislabelling is by 'another person' there is a defence. What this defence envisages, no doubt, is the mislabelling by say a mischievous stranger, but *Tesco* managed to convince the House of Lords that it also applied to the act of a junior employee. In arriving at this decision the Law Lords managed, of course, to undermine the Trade Descriptions Act. Nevertheless it must not be forgotten that *Tesco v Nattrass* is equally a statutory interpretation case and thus much depends upon the statute in issue.

Jetiva SA v Bilta (UK) Ltd [2015] UKSC 23 Supreme Court

Lord Toulson and Lord Hodge: ... **193.** As in each case the court is engaged in the interpretation of a particular statute and in its application to particular facts, other statutory provisions have given rise to different approaches. Thus in *Tesco Stores Ltd v Brent London Borough Council* [1993] 1 WLR 1037 the Divisional Court was concerned with the offence in section 11 of the Video Recordings Act 1984 of supplying a video recording to a person under the age specified in the classification certificate. The court rejected Tesco's statutory defence that it had neither known nor had reasonable grounds to believe that the purchaser was under 18. It distinguished *Tesco Supermarkets Ltd v Nattrass*, holding that the knowledge or information that the section 11(2) defence addressed was that of the employee who supplied the video film to the purchaser and not that of the company's senior management.

However this whole question of whether a criminal act of an employee is to be treated as the act of the company has raised difficult questions not just in criminal law, but in contract and tort cases as well.

In re Supply of Ready Mixed Concrete (No 2) [1995] 1 AC 456
House of Lords

Lord Templeman: ... The first principle is that a company is an entity separate from its members but, not being a physical person is only capable of acting by its agents. The second principle is that a company, in its capacity as supplier of goods, like any other person in the capacity of taxpayer, landlord or in any other capacity, falls to be judged by its actions and not by its language. An employee who acts for the company within the scope of his employment is the company. Directors may give instructions, top management may exhort, middle management may question and workers may listen attentively. But if a worker makes a defective product or a lower manager accepts or rejects an order, he is the company.

What amounts to 'scope of employment'? What if an employee of a company commits a crime: does this automatically take the employee outside of the 'scope'? The reasoning in *Tesco* suggests that it might; the employee becomes another person. But in private law the position is not so simple.

***Photo Production Ltd v Securicor Transport Ltd* [1980] AC 827**
House of Lords

Lord Wilberforce: My Lords, this appeal arises from the destruction by fire of the respondents' factory involving loss and damage agreed to amount to £615,000. The question is whether the appellant is liable to the respondents for this sum. ...

The duty of Securicor was, as stated, to provide a service. There must be implied an obligation to use due care in selecting their patrolmen, to take care of the keys and, I would think, to operate the service with due and proper regard to the safety and security of the premises. The breach of duty committed by Securicor lay in a failure to discharge this latter obligation. Alternatively it could be put upon a vicarious responsibility for the wrongful act of Musgrove – viz, starting a fire on the premises: Securicor would be responsible for this upon the principle stated in *Morris v. C W Martin Sons Ltd* [1966] 1 QB 716, 739. ...

Lord Diplock: ... My Lords, it is characteristic of commercial contracts, nearly all of which today are entered into not by natural legal persons, but by fictitious ones, ie companies, that the parties promise to one another that some thing will be done; for instance, that property and possession of goods will be transferred, that goods will be carried by ship from one port to another, that a building will be constructed in accordance with agreed plans, that services of a particular kind will be provided. Such a contract is the source of primary legal obligations upon each party to it to procure that whatever he has promised will be done is done. (I leave aside arbitration clauses which do not come into operation until a party to the contract claims that a primary obligation has not been observed.)

Where what is promised will be done involves the doing of a physical act, performance of the promise necessitates procuring a natural person to do it; but the legal relationship between the promisor and the natural person by whom the act is done, whether it is that of master and servant, or principal and agent, or of parties to an independent subcontract, is generally irrelevant. If that person fails to do it in the manner in which the promisor has promised to procure it to be done, as, for instance, with reasonable skill and care, the promisor has failed to fulfil his own primary obligation. This is to be distinguished from 'vicarious liability' – a legal concept which does depend upon the existence of a particular legal relationship between the natural person by whom a tortious act was done and the person sought to be made vicariously liable for it. In the interests of clarity the expression should, in my view, be confined to liability for tort. ...

Lord Salmon: ... The contract between the two parties provided that Securicor should supply a patrol service at Photo Production's factory by four visits a night for seven nights a week and two visits every Saturday afternoon and four day visits every Sunday. The contract provided that for this service, Securicor should be paid £8 15 a week. There can be no doubt that but for the clause in the contract which I have recited, Securicor would have been liable for the damage which was caused by their servant, Musgrove, whilst indubitably acting in the course of his employment: *Morris v. C W Martin Sons Ltd* [1966] 1 QB 716. …

Where a human person contracts with a fictional person (a corporation) the latter, as Lord Diplock points out, can only act through human beings, usually its employees or agents.

Yet the individualistic nature of criminal law can sometimes lead one into thinking that an employee who commits a crime during his employment ought not to 'infect' the company either with criminal liability or, on occasions at least, with contractual liability. However if a contract is made between a painter and a client for the former to paint a picture of the latter's house, can the painter himself escape liability if he fails to paint the picture blaming his fingers for not obeying his commands? One begins to see how this idea of a company being a fictional person can give rise to some serious reasoning problems.

Jetiva SA v Bilta (UK) Ltd [2015] UKSC 23 Supreme Court

Lord Mance: … **42.** Where the relevant rule consists in the duties owed by an officer to the company which he or she serves, then, whether such duties are statutory or common law, the acts, knowledge and states of mind of the company must necessarily be separated from those of its officer. The purpose of the rule itself means that the company cannot be identified with its officers. It is self-evidently impossible that the officer should be able to argue that the company either committed or knew about the breach of duty, simply because the officer committed or knew about it. This is so even though the officer is the directing mind and will of the company. The same clearly also applies even if the officer is also the sole shareholder of a company in or facing insolvency. Any other conclusion would ignore the separate legal identity of the company, empty the concept of duty of content and enable the company's affairs to be conducted in fraud of creditors.

43. At the same time, however, if the officer's breach of duty has led to the company incurring loss in the form of payments to or liability towards third parties, the company must be able as part of its cause of action against its officer to rely on the fact that, in that respect, its officer's acts and state of mind were and are attributable to the company, causing it to make such payments or incur such liability. In other words, it can rely on attribution for one purpose, but disclaim attribution for another. The rules of attribution for the purpose of establishing or negating vicarious liability to third parties differ, necessarily, from the rules governing the direct relationship inter se of the principal and agent.

Lord Sumption: … **65.** English law might have taken the position that a company, being an artificial legal construct, was mindless. If it had done that, then legal wrongs which depended on proof of some mental element such as dishonesty or intention could never be attributed to a company and the present question could not arise. In the early years of English company law, there were powerful voices which denied that a tort dependent on proof of a mental element could be committed by a company. For many years this view was principally associated with Lord Bramwell, who in a well-known dictum in *Abrath v North Eastern Railway Co* [1886] 11 App Cas 247, 250–251, declared that a fictitious person was 'incapable of malice or of motive' even if the whole body of its directors or shareholders in general meeting approved its acts for improper reasons. This question was, however, settled as far as English civil law was concerned by the end of the nineteenth century. As Lord Lindley put it in *Citizens' Life Assurance Co Ltd v Brown* [1904] AC 423, 426, once companies were recognised by the law as legal persons, they were liable to have the mental states of agents and employees such as dishonesty or malice attributed to them for the purpose of establishing civil liability. In the criminal law, the notion that a corporation was incapable of committing an offence requiring mens rea persisted rather longer. It was asserted in both the first edition (1909) and the second edition (1933) of *Halsbury's Laws of England*. But it was rejected in a series of decisions in 1944: see *Director of Public Prosecutions v Kent and Sussex Contractors Ltd* [1944] KB 146; *R v ICR Haulage Ltd* [1944] KB 551; *Moore v I Bresler Ltd* [1944] 2 All ER 515. It is now well established that a company can be indicted for conspiracy to defraud (*R v ICR Haulage Ltd* [1944] KB 551) or manslaughter before statute intervened in 2007 (*Attorney-General's Reference (No 2 of 1999)* [2000] QB 796), provided that an agent with the relevant state of mind can be sufficiently identified with it. It cannot be emphasised too strongly that neither in the civil nor in the criminal context does this involve piercing the corporate veil. It is simply a recognition of the fact that the law treats a company as thinking through agents, just as it acts through them. ...

70. The search for a test of a company's direct or 'personal' liability has sometimes been criticised as a distraction or an artificial anthropomorphism, and it is certainly true that English law might have developed along other lines. As it is, the distinction between a liability which is direct or 'personal' and one which is merely vicarious is firmly embedded in our law and has had a considerable influence on the way it has developed in relation to both kinds of liability. Vicarious liability does not involve any attribution of wrongdoing to the principal. It is merely a rule of law under which a principal may be held strictly liable for the wrongdoing of someone else. This is one reason why the law has been able to impose it as broadly as it has. It extends far more widely than responsibility under the law of agency: to all acts done within the course of the agent's employment, however humble and remote he may be from the decision-making process, and even if his acts are unknown to the principal, unauthorised by him and adverse to his interest or contrary to his express instructions (*Lloyd v Grace Smith & Co* [1912] AC 716), indeed even if they are criminal (*Lister v Hesley Hall Ltd* [2002] 1 AC 215). Personal or direct liability, on the other hand, has always been fundamental to the application of rules of law which are founded on culpability as opposed to mere liability. One example, as Lord Hoffmann pointed out in *Meridian Global*, is provided by the rules governing criminal responsibility, which do not usually recognise vicarious responsibility. Another is the class of statutory provisions dependent on a company's personal misconduct, such as a shipowner's right to limit his liability for a loss which is not attributable to his 'personal act or omission': see article 4 of the Convention on Limitation of Liability for Maritime Claims (1976) (Merchant Shipping Act 1995, Schedule 7, Part I), a principle derived from the nineteenth century Merchant Shipping Acts of the United Kingdom. A third example is provided by the illegality defence, which the House of Lords held in *Stone & Rolls v Moore Stephens* [2009] 1 AC 1391 to apply only to direct and not to vicarious responsibility. It is, for example, the reason why public policy precludes recovery under a liability policy in respect of a criminal act where the insured's liability is personal or direct, but not where it is purely vicarious: *Lancashire County Council v Municipal Mutual Insurance Ltd* [1997] QB 897, 907. As cases like this illustrate, if the illegality defence were to be engaged merely by proof of a purely vicarious liability, it would apply irrespective of any question of attribution, to any case in which the human wrongdoer was acting within the scope of his employment. This would extend the scope of the defence far more widely than anything warranted by the demands of justice or the principle stated by Lord Mansfield. On the footing that the attribution of culpability is essential to the defence, the concept of a 'directing mind and will' remains valuable. It describes a person who can be identified with the company either generally or for the relevant purpose, as distinct from one for whose acts the company is merely vicariously liable.

The distinction between direct and vicarious liability can often give rise to difficulties. Indeed it was one of the issues in *Esso v Southport Corporation* (see 3.5). The claimant had put into the statement of claim that the company who owned the ship was vicariously liable for the negligence of the captain, but Denning LJ, using public nuisance, argued that it was directly liable because it could not prove that the nuisance happened without its fault. The House of Lords held that it was too late to claim that the company was directly liable in negligence, although this holding was arguably wrong in law since the claimant had pleaded public nuisance as a cause of action.

Companies are, then, non-human persons. Yet can one find the reverse situation: can one treat a human person as a non-human person? In the past one certainly found it with regard to 'outlaws'; the law regarded them as dead and thus each outlaw was no longer a *persona*. In Germany during the Nazi era Jewish people were regarded as non-persons; and in South Africa before the constitutional revolution certain racial groups were treated, if not as non-humans as such, as humans with fewer rights than other groups (effectively as half persons). This ability of the law and legal reasoners to play around with human personality has been the source of much controversy and will no doubt continue to create social conflicts. If the law decides to treat unborn children as full persons, then abortion will become murder with all the implications that this would have for women's choice. Here, of course, political bias becomes of importance.

4.7 EXCURSUS: *PERSONA* AND FICTION

The idea of human and non-human persons has been a continual theme in cinema – one thinks of *Blade Runner* (1982) – and was the subject of an extraordinary film by Alfred Hitchcock. *Vertigo* (1958) has some relevance for lawyers in the way that it uses the notion of *persona* in an abstract way.

Raymond Durgnat, *The Strange Case of Alfred Hitchcock*, Faber & Faber, 1974, pp 278–279

A long-lost schoolfriend, Gavin Elster, asks [Scottie] to keep his wife Madeleine under surveillance. Scottie's misgivings about taking on a psychiatric job give way to curiosity when he learns of Madeleine's belief that she is the reincarnation of her great great grandmother, Carlotta Valdes, a kept woman of the gracious Spanish days. On seeing Madeleine (Kim Novak) he falls in love with her, stalking her along her mysterious journeys between the department store, a portrait of her ancestor in the museum, a boarding house from which she vanishes (if she ever was there), and, eventually, a suicide attempt under the Golden Gate Bridge, soon after she begins to return his love. ...

... [H]e resolves to intervene effectively in Madeleine's delusions. When she dreams of a Spanish Mission in Carlotta's day, he takes her to it to prove that it still exists, almost unchanged, and that her 'forgotten memory' has nothing supernatural to it. In the livery stables they exchange their first kiss. But she hurries away from him to climb the mission tower. Struggling weakly through his vertigo, he mounts its staircase at a crawl, only to see her plunge to her death.

A coroner accuses him of moral, if not legal, negligence, and he slumps into a catatonic state from which he gradually emerges, only to suffer from hallucinations provoked by women with the vaguest resemblance to his lost love. In the street outside 'Madeleine's' department store he meets a shopgirl, Judy (Kim Novak), who under the vulgarity and bitterness is her double. Her initial response is a scathing rejection of a corny pick-up, but sensing the force of his attachment she relents, and, like her predecessor, begins to return his love. But his love is for the original, and he has no sexual desire for her until she has perfected the resemblance; and as they kiss in her apartment, he hallucinates himself back into the livery stable, with the other. ...

It is uncertain, indeed, how far Scottie sees Judy as Madeleine returned or another Madeleine. Casually, carelessly, she dons the jewel which, completing the circle, breaks the spell. ...

Hitchcock's *Vertigo* skilfully uses *persona* and image. The viewer is told (by way of flashback), soon after Scottie meets Judy in the street, that Judy and Madeleine are the same person, Elster having played an elaborate trick on Scottie in order to murder his actual wife (who was the person who in truth fell from the bell tower). Yet the film is much more interested in Scottie's obsessive attempt to recreate 'Madeleine' using hair-style and clothes 'imposed' upon Judy.

Robin Wood, *Hitchcock's Films Revisited*, Columbia University Press, Revised Edition, 2002, p 123

... [I]n a sense, it is Madeleine who is the more 'real' of the two, since in Madeleine all kinds of potentialities completely hidden in Judy find expression. The pretence was that Carlotta was taking possession of Madeleine; in reality, Madeleine has taken possession of Judy ...

An added layer of personality is of course to be found in cinema itself. It uses actors to play particular characters and, indeed, the Latin word *persona* is said to have derived from masks used in Greek theatre. A single actor would play different people by changing masks. Thus in *Vertigo* there is an actress, Kim Novak, playing Judy who in turn is playing Madeleine who in turn is playing Carlotta. Personality becomes an almost abstract notion in this film and this is what makes it relevant to legal thinking. What is happening in *Vertigo* is a coming together – a merging – of the 'representor' with the thing 'represented'. Kim Novak, in playing two distinct characters, merges with them both just as the two characters merge in Kim Novak's Judy (or is it Madeleine?). Yet when analysing what is going on in the film one needs to distinguish Madeleine from Judy even though both, at the level of 'reality' (Kim Novak) and of the fictional narrative (Judy and Madeleine), are one and the same. This is rather like the legal corporation whose personality must be continually merged and yet differentiated from the personality of its individual human members (see in particular Lord Sumption, above, para 70).

One danger is that legal reasoners begin to believe that the legal corporation – the fiction – has a real personality (as Scottie believed that there was a real Madeleine).

***Jameel (Mohammed) v Wall Street Journal* [2007] 1 AC 359**
House of Lords

Lord Scott: ... **126.** And, in particular, I can see nothing in article 10 of the European Convention on Human Rights that requires a different conclusion. The right to freedom of expression was never intended, in my opinion, to allow defamatory statements, whether of individuals or companies, to be published with impunity. If a defamer can neither justify the statement nor claim the protection afforded by the law to fair comment on matters of public interest or to

> statements that qualify for privilege, he must, in my opinion, be prepared to answer for the libel. ...

Lord Scott seems to be suggesting that companies have human rights. Yet are companies *human*? However, not all of the judges in the case were prepared to treat companies as if they were like real people.

> ***Jameel (Mohammed) v Wall Street Journal*** **[2007] 1 AC 359**
> **House of Lords**
>
> **Lord Hoffmann** (dissenting on the proof of damage issue): ... **91.** In the case of an individual, his reputation is a part of his personality, the 'immortal part' of himself and it is right that he should be entitled to vindicate his reputation and receive compensation for a slur upon it without proof of financial loss. But a commercial company has no soul and its reputation is no more than a commercial asset, something attached to its trading name which brings in customers. I see no reason why the rule which requires proof of damage to commercial assets in other torts, such as malicious falsehood, should not also apply to defamation.

One might note that Lord Hoffman's view has now prevailed: Defamation Act 2013 s 1.

Another aspect of *Vertigo* is the role of a *res* – an object or thing – which links all of the female personalities in the film. This object is a brooch worn by Carlotta (in the painting of her) and which seemed to be in the possession of Madeleine. It is the object that finally, and suddenly, reveals to Scottie that Judy and Madeleine are one and the same, for Judy inadvertently (or perhaps not) puts it on while dressing for dinner. *Vertigo* is thus a film that uses the structure of relations between *personae* and *res* to create a narrative and this is where there is a similarity between film maker and judge.

4.8 IMAGE: CONSTRUCTION AND REPRESENTATION (REPRESENTATION THEORY)

What film and law share is that they both depict people and things. This depiction forms the basis of what might be termed representation theory.

Henry Bacon, Representation, in E Branigan and W Buckland (eds), *The Routledge Encyclopedia of Film Theory*, Routledge, 2014, 402, p 402

Representation is the depiction of things, classes, relationships, experiences, and other phenomena by means such as signs, images, models, formulas, and narratives. In an important sense the notion of representation – something standing for something else – implies that the real world is not simply out there for us to perfectly copy or experience without mediation. We assume material reality exists irrespective of our consciousness but only representations enable us to create a meaningful and workable relationship to that reality.

A point Paul Ricoeur has made about *mimesis* applies to representation. He thinks of *mimesis* not merely as an 'imitation' of reality (as the word has usually been translated) but, rather, as a creative act through which attention is focused on certain features of a thing by making them salient in terms of a particular way of modelling our perception and experience …

Lawyers and judges use persons and things to construct narratives – as indeed we have seen in some cases already examined – in order to underpin their reasoning.

Sometimes this *persona* and *res* construction can be quite subtle. A school girl is seriously injured during a school swimming session being conducted in a swimming pool that does not belong to the school. Should the school be liable for the negligence of the swimming instructor who is not an employee of the school?

***Woodland v Essex County Council* [2013] 3 WLR 853 Court of Appeal**

Laws LJ: … **26.** … The judge below also gave an example (paragraph 55) of a school outing to a zoo. Mishaps such as an accident in the bus on the way, or an animal bite at the zoo, would not expose the school to liability where the respective causes were the negligence of the bus driver and the zookeeper. The accident *en route* calls to mind a case in which the judgment was supplied to us by counsel after the argument was concluded: *Myton v Woods* (1980) WL 149543, in which a child had been injured on his way home from school, transport having been provided by the local authority. This court held that the council's duty was discharged by their having engaged a taxi firm: they were not liable for the driver's negligence.

Tomlinson LJ: … **57.** … Provided that undertaking a trip to the zoo in question did not itself amount to negligence because, for example, of the known incompetence with which the zoo is run, or, possibly, its lack of adequate liability insurance, I do not consider that we have been given any justification for such an outcome. Furthermore, the imposition of such liability would be likely, I think, to have a chilling effect on the willingness of education authorities to provide valuable educational experiences for their pupils.

The Court of Appeal said that the school should not be liable. Why? Because a swimming trip is just like (image) a trip to the zoo. However the decision was reversed in the Supreme Court where a different image was constructed.

Woodland v Swimming Teachers Association [2014] AC 537
Supreme Court

Lady Hale: ... **30.** Consider the cases of three 10-year-old children, Amelia, Belinda and Clara. Their parents are under a statutory duty to ensure that they receive efficient full-time education suitable to their age, ability and aptitude, and to any special needs they may have (Education Act 1996, section 7). Amelia's parents send her to a well-known and very expensive independent school. Swimming lessons are among the services offered and the school contracts with another school which has its own swimming pool to provide these. Belinda's parents send her to a large school run by a local education authority which employs a large sports staff to service its schools, including swimming teachers and life-guards. Clara's parents send her to a small state-funded faith school which contracts with an independent service provider to provide swimming lessons and life-guards for its pupils. All three children are injured during a swimming lesson as a result (it must be assumed) of the carelessness either of the swimming teachers or of the life-guards or of both. Would the man on the underground be perplexed to learn that Amelia and Belinda can each sue their own school for compensation but Clara cannot? ...

This is quite subtle 'image' reasoning because Lady Hale is offering a very different image in terms of persons (school girls) and things (schools) than the zoo and taxi images used by the Court of Appeal. The judges in this lower court used the image of a school (person) and zoo (thing) to show that there could not possibly be any liability on the part of the school for any negligence of a zoo official. Of course none of the judges could be said to be image-makers quite at the Hitchcockian level, but they are still able to create visual situations that are striking in terms of how they wish to justify their decisions. The differing images are important in understanding the mental processes behind judging. Different images result in different decisions. Yet this 'non-symbolic' form of knowledge representation in law is only now beginning to be the subject of serious research.

Marie-Laure Mathieu, _Les représentations dans la pensée des juristes_, IRJS Éditions, 2014, p 202 (translation Geoffrey Samuel)

The risk of failing to distinguish between the means of representation and the thing represented is particularly high in law, for the frontier is not so clear or so

> impermeable between reality and the representation of it. This risk becomes more intense when the author of the discourse has the power to 'mould' brute fact, as is the case with the judge ... as is the case [also] of the author who hopes that his theory, which is only ever a representation, and sometimes a representation without object, will finally be accepted as a real object by the scientific community.

In other words whether or not, say, the female claimant in *Miller v Jackson* (see 4.2) was 'obsessive' was not something necessarily rooted in 'brute fact' but perhaps was an image 'moulded' by two of the judges.

FURTHER READING AND QUESTIONS

1. On American Realism see Twining (1985) and on the construction of facts and non-symbolic knowledge see Samuel (2003). With regard to representation theory and cinema the work of Raymond Durgnat, despite the fact that he would not have wanted to be associated with theory, contains many excellent insights, especially in Durgnat (1967). A useful book on *Vertigo* is Barr (2002). A fundamental work on gender and legal reasoning is Hunter, McGlynn and Rackley (2010); this book should certainly be studied in relation to this chapter.
2. 'In any case, the passage from the general rule – or from the anterior decision – to the solution of the concrete case cannot be analysed in terms of a simple deductive application process; the subsumption of the case under the rule involves the intervention of a multitude of circumstances, elements and variables which prevent any claim to predict with certainty its result. Among these multiple givens always somewhat divergent, debatable and indeterminate, where is the truth with respect to the so-called positive law?' (Atias, 1994, 119). Discuss.
3. Try to watch *Vertigo* and then imagine the following scenario. Scottie actually marries Madeleine before her apparent mortal fall from the tower. He subsequently meets Judy in the street and they develop their relationship as in the film. Would it be true to say that Scottie and Judy are legally married, even though Scottie is not yet aware that Madeleine and Judy are the same person? Write a reasoned legal judgment.

5. The relationship between the official and unofficial portraits (1)

How do the official and unofficial portraits relate to each other in terms of legal knowledge? Much of course depends upon what one means by 'legal' in this context; but it is possible to identify three different positions that might help answer this question. Legal reasoning can, first, be examined from the position of a lawyer operating squarely within the discipline of law. Secondly, legal reasoning can be approached partly from within and partly from outside the discipline of law. A legal theorist may adopt, say, a viewpoint from another discipline such as economics or philosophy; or he/she may adopt, in part, a sociological position. Thirdly, legal reasoning can be examined from a position wholly outside the discipline of law. A social scientist might turn his/her attention to law, lawyers and the reasoning they use and perhaps employ a conceptual framework that is very different from the one used by a jurist examining legal reasoning from within the discipline of law. The first and the third position can be seen as operating under different 'paradigms'. There is what might be called an 'authority paradigm' which governs those operating within the discipline of law; and there is an 'inquiry paradigm' that motivates scientists and many social scientists.

5.1 AUTHORITY PARADIGM

As to the first – the authority paradigm – it has a connection with theology.

> **Karen Armstrong, 'Unholy strictures', *The Guardian*, 11 August 2005**
>
> Human beings, in nearly all cultures, have long engaged in a rather strange activity. They have taken a literary text, given it special status and attempted to live according to its precepts. These texts are usually of considerable antiquity yet they are expected to throw light on situations that their authors could not have imagined. In times of crisis, people turn to their scriptures with renewed zest and, with much creative ingenuity, compel them to speak to their current predicament. We are seeing a great deal of scriptural activity at the moment.

This comment by a theologian captures the spirit of the authority paradigm. Some texts have such authority that they cannot be criticised, only interpreted. Legal texts are a little like this. Of course a legal text can be criticised for its style and indeed for its content; one does not have to agree with the content of a legislative provision or a judgment in a case. But such texts cannot be dismissed, for they have the authority of the law. The law is the law.

Geoffrey Samuel, Interdisciplinarity and the Authority Paradigm: Should Law Be Taken Seriously by Scientists and Social Scientists? (2009) 36 *Journal of Law and Society* 431, p 437 (footnotes omitted)

Secondly, law as a discipline is regarded by many within the European tradition as having as its object rules or norms. Such rules or norms, once they are constitutionally valid, have an absolute authority. The academic commentator can criticise their content, their social effects, their drafting, their lack of coherence or their style; equally any decision rendered by a court of law can be criticised on similar grounds. But what cannot normally be disputed is their status as 'law'. The text and court decision have an absolute authority and thus an important aspect of law as a discipline – and one that it shares with theology – is that it is a subject that imposes upon itself an *auctoritas* paradigm.

When judging and legal reasoning are approached from within the discipline of law – from within the 'authority paradigm' – the tendency is to give an account of judging and reasoning that conforms to the expectations of those within the discipline.

***Home Office v Dorset Yacht Co Ltd* [1970] AC 1004 House of Lords**

Lord Diplock: ... The method adopted at this stage of the process is analytical and inductive. It starts with an analysis of the characteristics of the conduct and relationship involved in each of the decided cases. But the analyst must know what he is looking for; and this involves his approaching his analysis with some general conception of conduct and relationships which ought to give rise to a duty of care. This analysis leads to a proposition which can be stated in the form: 'In all the decisions that have been analysed a duty of care has been held to exist wherever the conduct and the relationship possessed each of the characteristics A, B, C, D etc, and has not so far been found to exist when any of these characteristics were absent.'

For the second stage, which is deductive and analytical, that proposition is converted to: 'In all cases where the conduct and relationship possess each of the characteristics A, B, C, D etc., a duty of care arises.' The conduct and relationship involved in the case for decision is then analysed to ascertain whether they possess each of these characteristics. If they do the conclusion follows that a duty of care does arise in the case for decision.

But since *ex hypothesi* the kind of case which we are now considering offers a choice whether or not to extend the kinds of conduct or relationships which give rise to a duty of care, the conduct or relationship which is involved in it will lack at least one of the characteristics A, B, C, or D etc. And the choice is exercised by making a policy decision … which … will be influenced by the same general conception of what ought to give rise to a duty of care as was used in approaching the analysis. The choice to extend is given effect to by redefining the characteristics in more general terms so as to exclude the necessity to conform to limitations imposed by the former definition which are considered to be inessential. …

Inherent in this methodology, however, is a practical limitation which is imposed by the sheer volume of reported cases. The initial selection of previous cases to be analysed will itself eliminate from the analysis those in which the conduct or relationship involved possessed characteristics which are obviously absent in the case for decision. The proposition used in the deductive stage is not a true universal. It needs to be qualified so as to read: 'In all cases where the conduct and relationship possess each of the characteristics A, B, C and D etc, but do not possess any of the characteristics Z, Y or X etc, which were present in the cases eliminated from the analysis, a duty of care arises.' But this qualification, being irrelevant to the decision of the particular case, is generally left unexpressed. …

From the previous decisions of the English courts … it is possible to arrive by induction at an established proposition of law as respects one of those special-relations: viz A is responsible for damage caused to the person or property of B by the tortious act of C (a person responsible in law for his own acts) where the relationship between A and C has the characteristics: (1) that A has the legal right to detain C in penal custody and to control his acts while in custody; (2) that A is actually exercising his legal right of custody of C at the time of C's tortious act; and (3) that A if he had taken reasonable care in the exercise of his right of custody could have prevented C from doing the tortious act which caused damage to the person or property of B; and where also the relationship between A and B has the characteristics; (4) that at the time of C's tortious act A has the legal right to control the situation of B or his property as respects physical proximity to C; and (5) that A can reasonably foresee that B is likely to sustain damage to his person or property if A does not take reasonable care to prevent C from doing tortious acts of the kind which he did. …

Induction (going from the particular to the general) and deduction (going from the general to the particular) are often regarded as the basic tools of legal reasoning. As for induction, this is frequently to be found in legal reasoning.

Digest of Justinian Book 2 Title 14 (translation Geoffrey Samuel)

1 ULPIAN, Edict, book 4. … 3. Agreement (*conventio*) is a general word applying to all things about which persons who deal with each other agree by contracting (*contrahendi*) or compromising a dispute (*transigendi*); for just as two people are said to come together when they are brought together and come to a single place from different locations, so also when people of different minds agree as one, that is come together in one mind. So general is the term agreement (*conventio*) Pedius makes the nice point that there can be no contract and no obligation, either made by the transfer of a thing (*re*) or by words, if not involving agreement; for even a stipulation which is made by words, without having agreement, is void. 4. But most agreements are formed under some name, for example sale, hire, pledge or stipulation.

Roman law did not have a law of contract, but a law of contracts. There were different kinds of contracts as Ulpian indicates. However the jurists induced out of these different contracts a common denominator, namely 'agreement' (*conventio*). There are many examples of this kind of inductive reasoning to be found in the common law.

Lloyds Bank Ltd v Bundy [1975] QB 326 Court of Appeal

Lord Denning MR: … Yet there are exceptions to this general rule. There are cases in our books in which the courts will set aside a contract, or a transfer of property, when the parties have not met on equal terms – when the one is so strong in bargaining power and the other so weak – that, as a matter of common fairness, it is not right that the strong should be allowed to push the weak to the wall. Hitherto those exceptional cases have been treated each as a separate category in itself. But I think the time has come when we should seek to find a principle to unite them. I put on one side contracts or transactions which are voidable for fraud or misrepresentation or mistake. All those are governed by settled principles. I go only to those where there has been inequality of bargaining power, such as to merit the intervention of the court. …

Gathering all together, I would suggest that through all these instances there runs a single thread. They rest on 'inequality of bargaining power.' By virtue of it, the English law gives relief to one who, without independent advice, enters into a contract upon terms which are very unfair or transfers property for a consideration which is grossly inadequate, when his bargaining power is grievously impaired by reason of his own needs or desires, or by his own ignorance or infirmity, coupled with undue influences or pressures brought to bear on him by or for the benefit of the other. When I use the word 'undue' I do not mean to suggest that the principle depends on proof of any wrongdoing. The one who stipulates for an unfair advantage may be moved solely by his own self-interest, unconscious of the distress he is bringing to the other. I have also avoided any reference to the will of the one being 'dominated' or 'overcome' by the other. One who is in extreme need may knowingly consent to a most improvident bargain, solely to relieve the straits in which he finds himself. Again, I do not mean to suggest that every transaction is saved by independent advice. But the absence of it may be fatal. With these explanations, I hope this principle will be found to reconcile the cases. …

This principle induced out of the cases by Lord Denning was short-lived (it was denied subsequently in a House of Lords case), but it still provides an excellent example of inductive reasoning. As for deduction, this is associated with the syllogism and with the rule model, as we have seen (see 2.1).

In addition to inductive and deductive reasoning, a good legal reasoner also needs, it would seem, an 'analytical' ability.

Hunter v Canary Wharf Ltd [1997] AC 655 House of Lords

Lord Goff: ... Since preparing this opinion, I have had the opportunity of reading in draft the speech of my noble and earned friend, Lord Cooke of Thorndon, and I have noticed his citation of academic authority which supports the view that the right to sue in private nuisance in respect of interference with amenities should no longer be restricted to those who have an interest in the affected land. I would not wish it to be thought that I myself have not consulted the relevant academic writings. I have, of course, done so as is my usual practice; and it is my practice to refer to those which I have found to be of assistance, but not to refer, critically or otherwise, to those which are not. In the present circumstances, however, I feel driven to say that I found in the academic works which I consulted little more than an assertion of the desirability of extending the right of recovery in the manner favoured by the Court of Appeal in the present case. I have to say (though I say it in no spirit of criticism, because I know full well the limits within which writers of textbooks on major subjects must work) that I have found no analysis of the problem; and in circumstances such as this, a crumb of analysis is worth a loaf of opinion. Some writers have uncritically commended the decision of the Court of Appeal in *Khorasandjian v Bush* [1993] QB 727, without reference to the misunderstanding in *Motherwell v Motherwell*, 73 DLR (3d) 62, on which the Court of Appeal relied, or consideration of the undesirability of making a fundamental change to the tort of private nuisance to provide a partial remedy in cases of individual harassment. For these and other reasons, I did not, with all respect, find the stream of academic authority referred to by my noble and learned friend to be of assistance in the present case.

Quite what Lord Goff means by 'no analysis of the problem' is difficult to say, especially when compared to Lord Cooke's comment in the same case (see 3.8). Lord Goff seems to be contrasting analysis with opinion. Yet what is probably in issue is a conflict between schemes of intelligibility: the academic writers were welcoming *Khorasandjian v Bush* on the basis of a functional analysis while Lord Goff was searching for a conceptual and structural analysis (see 4.4).

In fact legal reasoning is not just about the analysis of precedents; an 'analysis' of the facts can be equally important.

***Blackpool & Fylde Aero Club Ltd v Blackpool Borough Council* [1990] 1 WLR 1195 Court of Appeal**

Bingham LJ: … A tendering procedure of this kind is, in many respects, heavily weighted in favour of the invitor. He can invite tenders from as many or as few parties as he chooses. He need not tell any of them who else, or how many others, he has invited. The invitee may often, although not here, be put to considerable labour and expense in preparing a tender, ordinarily without recompense if he is unsuccessful. The invitation to tender may itself, in a complex case, although again not here, involve time and expense to prepare, but the invitor does not commit himself to proceed with the project, whatever it is; he need not accept the highest tender; he need not accept any tender; he need not give reasons to justify his acceptance or rejection of any tender received. The risk to which the tenderer is exposed does not end with the risk that his tender may not be the highest or, as the case may be, lowest. But where, as here, tenders are solicited from selected parties all of them known to the invitor, and where a local authority's invitation prescribes a clear, orderly and familiar procedure – draft contract conditions available for inspection and plainly not open to negotiation, a prescribed common form of tender, the supply of envelopes designed to preserve the absolute anonymity of tenderers and clearly to identify the tender in question, and an absolute deadline – the invitee is in my judgment protected at least to this extent: if he submits a conforming tender before the deadline he is entitled, not as a matter of mere expectation but of contractual right, to be sure that his tender will after the deadline be opened and considered in conjunction with all other conforming tenders or at least that his tender will be considered if others are. Had the club, before tendering, inquired of the council whether it could rely on any timely and conforming tender being considered along with others, I feel quite sure that the answer would have been 'of course.' The law would, I think, be defective if it did not give effect to that. …

The approach of Bingham LJ is anything but deductive or even rule orientated. His reasoning is one that functions from inside the facts where he effects a sleight-of-hand jump from 'expectation' (a descriptive notion) to a 'right' (normative notion). One might categorise this approach as distinctly 'bottom-up' reasoning (*ex facto ius oritur*, said the medieval jurist Baldus). This is said to be very much the common law method.

***Roxborough v Rothmans of Pall Mall (Australia) Ltd* [2001] HCA 68, (2001) 208 C.L.R. 516 High Court of Australia**

Gummow J: … **72.** Considerations such as these, together with practical experience, suggest caution in judicial acceptance of any all-embracing theory of restitutionary rights and remedies founded upon a notion of 'unjust enrichment'. To the lawyer whose mind has been moulded by civilian influences, the theory may come first, and the source of the theory may be the writing of jurists not the decisions of judges. However, that is not the way in which a system based on case law develops; over time, general principle is derived from judicial decisions upon particular instances, not the other way around.

The common law method is, it seems, suspicious of deductive reasoning (but cf Conte, 2015). Analogy and induction are the preferred tools. However there is actually a philosophical – or more accurately an epistemological – issue behind this 'top-down' and 'bottom-up' reasoning.

Albert R Jonsen and Stephen Toulmin, *The Abuse of Casuistry*, University of California Press, 1988, p 19

... On the one hand, for some 2,500 years there have always been those who regarded ethics as a topic for *theoretical* discussion: a kind of 'moral geometry' that makes particular ethical perceptions more intelligible by showing how they exemplify rules or laws that are both *more general* and also capable of being known with *greater certainty*. This first view treats ethics as a science, which gives a coherent and systematic account of human conduct of a kind that our unsystematized moral perceptions can only hint at.

On the other hand, from the very beginning there have been other thinkers who challenged the adequacy of this first approach. Aristotle, for instance, questioned whether moral understanding lends itself to scientific systematization at all, ... Far from being based on general abstract principles that can at one and the same time be universal, invariable, and known with certainty (he argued), ethics deals with a multitude of particular concrete situations, which are themselves so variable that they resist all attempts to generalize about them in universal terms. In short, Aristotle declared, ethics is not and cannot be a science. Instead, it is a field of experience that calls for a recognition of significant particulars and for informed prudence: for what he called *phronesis*, or 'practical wisdom.' ...

Gummow J is perhaps giving expression to this idea that the common law is not a science. It is a law of practical wisdom. This in turn can be analysed in terms of two different kinds of reasoning.

Albert R Jonsen and Stephen Toulmin, *The Abuse of Casuistry*, University of California Press, 1988, pp 34–35

Theoretical arguments are structured in ways that free them from any dependence on the circumstances of their presentation and ensure them a *validity* of a kind that is not affected by the practical context of use. In formal arguments particular conclusions are deduced from ('entailed by') the initial axioms or universal principles that are the apex of the argument. So the truth or certainty that attaches to those axioms *flows downward* to the specific instances to be proved. ...

In the language of formal logic, the axioms are *major premises*, the facts that specify the present instance are *minor premises*, and the conclusion to be 'proved' is deduced (follows *necessarily*) from the initial premises.

Practical arguments, by contrast, involve a wider range of factors than formal deductions and are read with an eye to their occasion of use. Instead of aiming at strict entailments, they draw on the outcomes of previous experience, carrying over the procedures used to resolve earlier problems and reapplying them in new problematic situations. Practical arguments depend for their power on how closely the *present* circumstances resemble those of the earlier *precedent* cases for which this particular type of argument was originally devised. So, in practical arguments, the truths and certitudes established in the precedent cases *pass sideways*, so as to provide 'resolutions' of later problems. ...

Axiomatic or deductive reasoning can be contrasted with casuistic reasoning, the first being top down and the second being bottom up. The common law – and perhaps Roman and medieval law – are characterised by the latter (see 1.1 and 1.2) while the modern civil law is said to be characterised by the former (see 1.3).

5.2 AUTHORITY AND COHERENCE

Nevertheless, whatever the status of casuistic reasoning, some would argue that an important aspect of law's authority is coherence. Certainly, within the civil law tradition, coherence has, since the 16th century, been a fundamental means of epistemological validation; the more coherent a system of laws, the more authority it is said to display.

Christian Atias, *Épistémologie juridique*, Dalloz, 2002, pp 195–196, 197
(translation Geoffrey Samuel)

330 ... Nobody can doubt the influence that the preoccupation with coherence exercises on the constitution of legal knowledge. It is partly tied to the preference for simplicity, but it can be distinguished from this and goes beyond simplicity. Does not private law for example – in particular the law of obligations – gain its glory from this kind of harmony which permits the construction of fine theories? ...

334 ... A description of positive law can, for example, be said to be erroneous because it lacks the required coherence. This reference to coherence constitutes a criterion of truth. A legal solution to a problem can be characterised as being outside of the established law on the ground that it does not conform to a body of rules designed to protect certain interests over others; the solution is criticised as being in error because it goes against the established position confirmed on multiple occasions in the case law (*jurisprudence*). In confirming a recognised coherence, this '*jurisprudence*' defines the established legal position against which it is difficult to dissent. …

Professor Atias was, of course, talking of the civil law. But his words are echoed by some theorists in the common law world.

Andrew Robertson, Constraints on Policy-Based Reasoning in Private Law, in A Robertson and TH Wu (eds), *The Goals of Private Law*, Hart, 2009, p 271 (footnotes omitted)

Related to the doctrine of precedent is the notion that the courts are constrained by the formal legal goal of ensuring consistency between related principles and related bodies of law. …

Whether private law can accommodate policy considerations at all depends on the nature of the coherence that is required or, more precisely, what particular features of private law are required to cohere with each other. Weinrib argues that the need for coherence precludes policy-based reasoning altogether … Weinrib's notion of coherence requires symmetrical justifications for the plaintiff's right and the defendant's liability. Since policy considerations are always one-sided, the use of policy considerations always produces incoherence in the sense of asymmetry between the justifications underlying the plaintiff's right on the one hand and the defendant's obligation or liability on the other.

One might note the two different institutional models in play in this Robertson extract: the policy model of reasoning (see 3.3) in conflict with the rights model (see 3.1), the authority of coherence being employed to justify the formalist theory of rights as against the functionalist theory that underpins policy arguments.

However, the English judges have seemed much less interested in coherence as a means of justifying decisions.

***Read v J Lyons & Co* [1947] AC 156 House of Lords**

Lord Macmillan: … Your Lordships' task in this House is to decide particular cases between litigants and your Lordships are not called upon to rationalise the law of England. That attractive if perilous field may well be left to other hands to cultivate. It has been necessary in the present instance to examine certain general principles advanced on behalf of the appellant because it was said that consistency required that these principles should be applied to the case in hand. Arguments based on legal consistency are apt to mislead for the common law is a practical code adapted to deal with the manifold diversities of human life, and as a great American judge has reminded us, 'the life of the law has not been logic; it has been experience.' For myself, I am content to say that in my opinion no authority has been quoted from case or textbook which would justify your Lordships, logically or otherwise, in giving effect to the appellant's plea. I would accordingly dismiss the appeal.

'Practical justice' seems to be a stronger motivating factor as Lord Steyn indicated in *Att-Gen v Blake* (see 3.7).

5.3 AUTHORITY AND JUSTICE

Nevertheless this does not mean that coherence has no role; it depends upon the conception of justice that is brought into play.

***McFarlane v Tayside Health Board* [2000] 2 AC 59 House of Lords (Scotland)**

Lord Steyn: My Lords, A surgeon wrongly and negligently advised a husband and wife that a vasectomy had rendered the husband infertile. Acting on his advice they ceased to take contraceptive precautions. The wife became pregnant and gave birth to a healthy child. The question is what damages, if any, the parents are in principle entitled to recover. …

It is possible to view the case simply from the perspective of corrective justice. It requires somebody who has harmed another without justification to indemnify the other. On this approach the parents' claim for the cost of bringing up Catherine must succeed. But one may also approach the case from the vantage point of distributive justice. It requires a focus on the just distribution of burdens and losses among members of a society. If the matter is approached in this way, it may become relevant to ask commuters on the Underground the following question: Should the parents of an unwanted but healthy child be able to sue the doctor or hospital for compensation equivalent to the cost of bringing up the child for the years of his or her minority, i.e. until about 18 years? My Lords, I am firmly of the view that an overwhelming number of ordinary men and women would answer the question with an emphatic 'No.' And the reason for such a response would be an inarticulate premise as to what is morally acceptable and what is not. Like Ognall J in *Jones v Berkshire Area Health Authority* (unreported) 2 July 1986 they will have in mind that many couples cannot have children and others have the sorrow and burden of looking after a disabled child. The realisation that compensation for financial loss in respect of the upbringing of a child would necessarily have to discriminate between rich and poor would surely appear unseemly to them. It would also worry them that parents may be put in a position of arguing in court that the unwanted child, which they accepted and care for, is more trouble than it is worth. Instinctively, the traveller on the Underground would consider that the law of tort has no business to provide legal remedies consequent up upon the birth of a healthy child, which all of us regard as a valuable and good thing.

My Lords, to explain decisions denying a remedy for the cost of bringing up an unwanted child by saying that there is no loss, no foreseeable loss, no causative link or no ground reasonable restitution is to resort to unrealistic and formalistic propositions which mask the real reasons for the decisions. And judges ought to strive to give the real reasons for their decision. It is my firm conviction that where courts of law have denied a remedy for the cost of bringing up an unwanted child the real reasons have been grounds of distributive justice. That is, of course, a moral theory. It may be objected that the House must act like a court of law and not like a court of morals. That would only be partly right. The court must apply positive law. But judges' sense of the moral answer to a question, or the justice of the case, has been one of the great shaping forces of the common law. What may count in a situation of difficulty and uncertainty is not the subjective view of the judge but what he reasonably believes that the ordinary citizen would regard as right. ...

In my view it is legitimate in the present case to take into account considerations of distributive justice. That does not mean that I would decide the case on grounds of public policy. On the contrary, I would avoid those quick sands. Relying on principles of distributive justice I am persuaded that our tort law does not permit parents of a healthy unwanted child to claim the costs of bringing up the child from a health authority or a doctor. If it were necessary to do so, I would say that the claim does not satisfy the requirement of being fair, just and reasonable. ...

The rights model (see 3.1) emphasises the individual and thus it is underpinned by the corrective justice perspective. It is about justice between individuals. Distributive justice would, however, appear to be different from policy reasoning and so it is difficult to assert that it underpins the policy model (cf 3.3).

Yet policy reasoning tends to be orientated towards the social function of legal provisions and thus may not be irrelevant despite Lord Steyn's insistence on a distinction. This said, Lord Steyn also appealed to coherence.

***McFarlane v Tayside Health Board* [2000] 2 AC 59 House of Lords (Scotland)**

Lord Steyn: ... This conclusion is reinforced by an argument of coherence. There is no support in Scotland and England for a claim by a disadvantaged child for damage to him arising from his birth: see *McKay v. Essex Area Health Authority* [1982] 1 QB 1166. Given this position, which also prevails in Australia, Trinidade and Cane (*The Law of Torts in Australia*, 3rd ed, 434) observe: '... it might seem inconsistent to allow a claim by the parents while that of the child, whether healthy or disabled, is rejected. Surely the parents' claim is equally repugnant to ideas of the sanctity and value of human life and rests, like that of the child, on a comparison between a situation where a human being exists and one where it does not.' In my view this reasoning is sound. Coherence and rationality demand that the claim by the parents should also be rejected. ...

Coherence (at least in a loose sense) seems to be militating against policy reasoning. What, then, is the relationship between the authority paradigm and the policy model of reasoning?

5.4 AUTHORITY AND POLICY

There is certainly something of a conflict between coherence to be found in reasoning based on a formalist model (rules and/or rights) and reasoning based upon public policy. One problem with policy is that some litigation disputes generate conflicting policy considerations (see 3.3). In such a situation the authority paradigm seems to assert itself with the result that the judges are forced back onto other reasoning models.

***McFarlane v Tayside Health Board* [2000] 2 AC 59 House of Lords (Scotland)**

Lord Clyde (dissenting in part): ... The relevance of the pursuers' claims may be considered from various points of view. One approach is that of public policy. This has played a part in the development of the law in England in dealing with cases such as the present, and more prominently and extensively in the corresponding judicial decisions in the USA. But I have considerable difficulty in finding assistance towards the solution of the present problem by reference to considerations of policy. In the present context at least, what are referred to as policy considerations include elements of what may be seen as ethical or moral considerations. But whatever the label used to identify or describe them I am not persuaded that a sufficiently solid ground for decision in the circumstances of the present case can be found by searching for a reason in policy. For one thing it is difficult to find any 'policy' ground for upholding the pursuers' claim in whole or part without finding beside it a countervailing consideration which points to the propriety of disallowing the claim. This point has been developed by CR Symmons in '*Policy Factors in Actions for Wrongful Birth*' (1987) 50 MLR 269. To take but one example, the 'sanctity of human life' can be put forward as a ground for justifying the law's refusal of a remedy for a wrongful conception. On the other hand the general recognition of the importance of family planning in society and of the propriety of adopting methods of contraception including those involving a treatment designed to achieve a permanent solution, reflects the recognition that unlimited child-bearing is not necessarily a blessing and the propriety of imposing a liability on those who negligently provide such a treatment. Particularly where consideration of public policy can be invoked by both sides to the dispute, it seems to me that to proceed upon such a ground is unlikely to lead to any confident solution.

Furthermore while it is comforting to be able to affirm that one can see no policy reasons for not allowing a claim such as the present to succeed, that gives little basis in principle for justifying why it should succeed. And to affirm more positively that public policy requires that the claim should succeed seems to me to be coming very close to an encroachment on the responsibilities which attach to the legislature and not to the courts. The judicial function may extend beyond the interpretation of the law to the problem of applying the law to novel circumstances. But in doing so the court should have regard to existing principles. It may be that considerations of what may be referred to as policy are of assistance in determining whether the application of the law should be extended so as to create a novel liability for damages. But the problem in the present case is not truly that kind of question. It is a problem of determining the extent of the damages to which in the circumstances the defenders are liable in law.

Public policy was long ago recognised by Burrough J in *Richardson v. Mellish* (1824) 2 Bing 229, 252, as 'a very unruly horse, and when once you get astride of it you never know where it will carry you.' As Pearson J. observed in his dissent in *Public Health Trust v. Brown* (1980) 388 So. 1084, 1086 'I am confident that the majority recognises that any decision based upon notions of public policy is one about which reasonable persons may disagree.' In *In re Mirams* [1891] 1 QB 594, 595, Cave J observed that judges should be 'trusted [more] as interpreters of the law than as expounders of what is called public policy.' While there may be occasions on which the courts may safely enter so uncertain a territory, at least in the circumstances of the present case I do not consider that it is useful in the present case to pursue so uncertain and unpromising a line of approach. …

One might note the use of image (metaphor) of an 'unruly horse' to discredit policy reasoning. However, it might be valuable to recall that the distinction between legal principle and policy is by no means as easy to determine as one might think.

Stephen Waddams, *Principle and Policy in Contract Law: Competing or Complementary Concepts?*, Cambridge University Press, 2011, pp 20–21, 227

A historical study cannot show which linguistic usage is superior, or which approach would be preferable in an ideal legal system. But it can show that, over a considerable period of time in English contract law and in the law of related jurisdictions, the formulation of principles, in the sense of generalized justifying propositions, has very commonly been influenced by considerations of convenience, common sense, a general sense of what is just in the particular case and a judgment of what is desirable for the future … .

From a historical perspective contract law cannot be reduced to any single or simple explanatory idea, internal or external. The interdependence of principle and policy is part of the reason for this conclusion: every principle, since it incorporates prudential considerations, has operated in tension with countervailing considerations which themselves can be, and often have been, formulated as principles. …

In *McFarlane* the judges could have dismissed the claim simply on the basis of a clearly established rule, namely the pure economic loss rule of negligence. No mention of morals or policy need have been made. In other words a purely formalist analysis was open to the court, but it is clear that the judges consider such an approach inadequate.

5.5 AUTHORITY AND STRUCTURALISM

Indeed there was resistance to treating the case as one of categorisation.

***McFarlane v Tayside Health Board* [2000] 2 AC 59 House of Lords (Scotland)**

Lord Millett (dissenting in part): … I do not think that the solution is to be found in a process of categorisation, whether of the nature of the delict or the loss in respect of which damages are claimed. It is true that the claims in the present case are brought under the extended *Hedley Byrne* principle (*Hedley Byrne & Co. Ltd. v. Heller & Partners Ltd.* [1964] A.C. 465). But I agree with my noble and learned friend Lord Steyn that it should not matter whether the unwanted pregnancy arises from the negligent supply of incorrect information or from the negligent performance of the operation itself. It is also true that the claim for the costs of bringing up Catherine is a claim in respect of economic loss, and that claims in delict for pure economic loss are with good reason more tightly controlled than claims in respect of physical loss. But I do not consider that the present question should depend on whether the economic loss is characterised as pure or consequential. The distinction is technical and artificial if not actually suspect in the circumstances of the present case, and is to my mind made irrelevant by the fact that Catherine's conception and birth are the very things that the defenders' professional services were called upon to prevent. In principle any losses occasioned thereby are recoverable however they may be characterised. Moreover the distinction has no moral content, and while ostensibly relied upon by some of those who have rejected the claim it can in reality have played no part in their belief that it would be morally wrong to accede to it.

A 'technical and artificial' approach is not the way to deal with cases that do raise difficult policy considerations even if policy reasoning itself is to be rejected. Taxonomy and categorisation are, nevertheless, considered fundamental by some writers.

Peter Birks, Definition and Division: A Meditation on *Institutes* 3.13, in P Birks (ed), *The Classification of Obligations*, Oxford University Press, 1997, p 34

If then the law is destined in day-to-day reality to be context-based, and if the alphabet is ideally suited to the ordering of contextual subjects, can it be said that legal taxonomy matters at all? Does it matter whether we have a well-co-ordinated map of the law or of that very important part of it which we call the law of obligations? ... The danger is that one topic will cease to be able to speak to another, each one having developed its own technical language and its own view of the world. The topics have to use compatible software. They have to be able to talk to each other. And, if like cases are to be treated alike, it is essential to enable the work which is being done in any one category to avoid the contradictions and inconsistencies which are endemic when the law consists in heaps of isolated packages. ...

The development of 'compatible software' (note the image employed) goes back to the Roman jurist Gaius who (while unaware of 'software') produced, as we have seen (see 1.1), a coherent plan of the whole of private law (in the sense of fitting together as a whole). Indeed the groundwork was done by the generations of jurists before him. What is important about the Gaian 'institutional plan' is that, in the 16th century, it finally replaced the order of the *Digest* as the means of comprehending the whole of private law (see eg Doneau, *Commentarii de Jure Civili*, Book I, chap II, § 3). The plan is thus found as the structural basis of all the European civil codes. The plan was, and is, more than just a 'map' or structure of the law; it is also a system in that, like numbers, each element defines itself with reference to other elements. For example the moment one grants a legal action to a town the town itself becomes a legal subject, that is to say a 'person' (see 4.6). Equally if one protects some intangible asset with an *actio in rem* the asset becomes a form of property. This structural way of perceiving law and legal knowledge has been, and remains, of major importance, at least for academic lawyers if not for judges. As Sir Henry Maine said of the 16th- and 17th-century civil law jurists, reform of the law meant reform of the law books (Maine, 1890, 363). This kind of law reform is still practised by academic lawyers; and some see this form of structural categorisation as being fundamental to legal reasoning and the deciding of cases.

Eric Descheemaeker, *The Division of Wrongs: A Historical Comparative Study*, Oxford University Press, 2009, p 255

I am not concerned here with the fairness of the decision in *Spring*, but solely with taxonomical issues. The aim of this section ... is to show what might potentially happen, and in the case of *Spring* did actually happen, when the law resorts to a bent classification comprising intersecting categories; it is that the law will end up divided against itself. By construction, a negligent defamation is both negligent and defamatory. But what is the law about negligent defamatory statements? For the same injury (loss of earnings, seen as pure economic loss from the perspective of negligence and consequential economic loss from the perspective of defamation), one section of the law of wrongs will grant a remedy and another will deny it.

... At worst, as in *Spring*, it will undermine the rationality (and the authority) of the law by allowing contradictory results to co-exist. ...

Spring v Guardian Assurance Plc [1995] 2 AC 296 is an interesting case in that it can indeed be seen as involving the reputation interest, which in turn leads one towards the tort of defamation. Yet the claimant also suffered serious financial loss, which means that one can equally classify it under economic loss arising from a misstatement, thus bringing into play the *Hedley Byrne* principle (negligence), which protects economic interests in relationships that are often close to contract. A structural model (see 3.1) of the type envisaged by Dr Descheemaeker sees two areas of the law contradicting each other; an interest model (see 3.4), in contrast, sees certain interests protected when there is an undertaking by the defendant and reliance by the claimant (which is the situation in *Spring* where the harm was caused by a reference which was inaccurate). So, what does the authority paradigm demand? Does the authority paradigm insist that judges should classify the case under reputation and defamation rather than misstatement and negligence? The judges clearly do not seem to think so, but, unlike some academics, they are often more concerned with fairness than taxonomy (see reception theory below 6.6). Such an approach, says Dr Descheemaeker, undermines the rationality of the law and thus its authority (although Dr Descheemaeker offers no empirical evidence to support this loss of authority assertion). But is the authority of the law that dependent upon taxonomy? Can factual situations always be subsumed under just one category?

Stephen Waddams, *Dimensions of Private Law: Categories and Concepts in Anglo-American Legal Reasoning*, Cambridge University Press, 2003, p 14

No map or scheme could possibly classify all imaginable facts, for there is no limit whatever to the number of facts that may be postulated of a sequence of human events. The selection of legally relevant facts is a matter not of empirical investigation but of judgment, and not wholly separable from the formulation of the applicable legal rule. Facts are selected and marshalled to fit perceived rules of law, but the rules themselves change in response to facts, often by deploying concepts and categories that had not formerly been supposed to be applicable.

A vaguely similar taxonomy problem arose in contract where a key classification distinction within this subject is the one between a contract to supply goods and a contract to supply a service. In the former contract if the goods supplied turn out to be defective the seller is strictly liable; he/she is, thanks to statute, impliedly promising to supply fit goods of satisfactory quality and it is no defence to show that the seller was not at fault (see eg Sale of Goods Act 1979 s 14; Consumer Rights Act 2015 ss 9–10). With the supply of a service the position is different. The business supplier impliedly promises only to use his/her best skill and thus will not be in breach of contract unless fault can be shown (Supply of Goods and Services Act 1982 s 13; Consumer Rights Act 2015 s 49). In civil law thinking the distinction is said to be an obligation of result as contrasted with one of means (see *Unidroit Principles for International Commercial Contracts* art 5.1.4). However, English judges do not feel themselves always bound by this goods and services classification.

***Platform Funding Ltd v Bank of Scotland* [2009] QB 426 Court of Appeal**

Rix LJ: ... **51.** Of course, like any distinction drawn by the law for the purpose of fairly and accurately articulating the briefly stated arrangements of mankind, it is possible to think of more or less difficult cases which challenge the issue of which side of the line a particular decision should fall on. What, therefore, of the examples canvassed before us of the surveyor who inspects the right property but errs in the extent of the garden which applies to it? Or of the surveyor who fails to visit all the rooms or spaces in a property? Or of the surveyor who inspects the wrong flat in a house? I am not deterred by such examples. I have an untutored opinion about each of them, but would prefer to leave such cases to be argued on their particular facts. I do not think that they displace the intuitive and common-sense view that the inspection of the wrong property, like the painting of the wrong portrait, or the photographing of the wrong wedding, is a straightforward breach of retainer and contract, and one which does not depend on the taking or absence of reasonable care. ...

There is choice, then, within the authority paradigm and the common law judges have for the most part resisted any attempt to impose on them a system of judging and reasoning founded upon a closed conceptual structure of concepts and rules to be applied strictly through syllogistic reasoning. The life of the common law has not been logic. Nevertheless structuralism remains a fundamental epistemological scheme of intelligibility for understanding the phenomenon of law.

5.6 AUTHORITY AS RESTRAINT

A structural view of law aims inter alia at reducing uncertainty in legal decision making, but previous chapters have indicated that there is a large element of choice when it comes to judging, decision making, and reasoning. Just how much choice there is – or should be – is a debate that is almost as old as law itself. Several restraints that have been openly expressed by judges are these. The first is stability.

> ***Rees v Darlington Memorial Hospital NHS Trust* [2004] 1 AC 309**
> **House of Lords**
>
> **Lord Bingham**: ... **7.** I am of the clear opinion, for reasons more fully given by my noble and learned friends, that it would be wholly contrary to the practice of the House to disturb its unanimous decision in *McFarlane* given as recently as four years ago, even if a differently constituted committee were to conclude that a different solution should have been adopted. It would reflect no credit on the administration of the law if a line of English authority were to be disapproved in 1999 and reinstated in 2003 with no reason for the change beyond a change in the balance of judicial opinion. I am not in any event persuaded that the arguments which the House rejected in 1999 should now be accepted, or that the policy considerations which (as I think) drove the decision have lost their potency. Subject to one gloss, therefore, which I regard as important, I would affirm and adhere to the decision in *McFarlane*.

One might note Lord Bingham's observation that a differently constituted court might have arrived at a different result in *McFarlane*. It is difficult to imagine a French judge saying this, at least in public. The legislator in the civilian systems (or some of them) is the one who has supposedly judged while the judges are administrators simply applying the texts.

The second restraint is the audience, which includes not just lawyers.

> ***Woodland v Swimming Teachers Association* [2014] AC 537 Supreme Court**
>
> **Lady Hale**: ... **29.** It is also important, so far as possible, that the distinctions produced by this process make sense to ordinary people. They should not, as Lord Steyn observed in *White v Chief Constable of South Yorkshire Police* [1999] 2 AC 455, 495, produce 'an imbalance in the law of tort which might perplex the man on the underground'. In that case, their Lordships obviously thought that the public would be perplexed if the police officers who were present at the Hillsborough disaster could claim compensation for the psychiatric harm they had suffered as a result of the negligence of their fellow officers when the spectators who had suffered the same harm for the same reason could not. In this case we have the reverse situation, where the public might well be perplexed if one pupil could sue her school for injuries sustained during a negligently conducted swimming lesson but another could not.

This involvement of the public – indirectly of course – in judging acts both as a restraint and as a means for change. It can be a reason for rethinking the established law.

However the public reaction may have to cede to a third restraint, which is principle.

> ***Rees v Darlington Memorial Hospital NHS Trust* [2004] 1 AC 309 House of Lords**
>
> **Lord Steyn** (dissenting): ... **46.** Like Lord Hope I regard the idea of a conventional award in the present case as contrary to principle. It is a novel procedure for judges to create such a remedy. There are limits to permissible creativity for judges. In my view the majority have strayed into forbidden territory. It is also a backdoor evasion of the legal policy enunciated in *McFarlane*. If such a rule is to be created it must be done by Parliament. The fact is, however, that it would be a hugely controversial legislative measure. It may well be that the Law Commissions and Parliament ought in any event, to consider the impact of the creation of a power to make a conventional award in the cases under consideration for the coherence of the tort system. ...

This restraint exercised by principle no doubt overlaps with stability. But as Lord Steyn indicates it can have a direct restraining force on judicial creativity.

5.7 AUTHORITY AND EVIDENCE

It has already been seen how important facts are in the judging process (see 4.2 and 4.3). Another aspect of judging that operates at the level of facts is their proof. In private (as opposed to criminal) law a claimant normally has to prove a fact on the balance of probabilities (more than 50 per cent). Often causation is central: a claimant has to prove, as a fact, that the damage has been caused by the defendant. This can evidently be a great restraint on claimants even where the law itself appears clear. When causation proves difficult to prove, how do the judges reason?

Milton Keynes BC v Nulty [2013] 1 WLR 1183 Court of Appeal

Toulson LJ: ... **35.** The civil 'balance of probability' test means no less and no more than that the court must be satisfied on rational and objective grounds that the case for believing that the suggested means of causation occurred is stronger than the case for not so believing. In the USA the usual formulation of this standard is a 'preponderance of the evidence'. In the British Commonwealth the generally favoured term is a 'balance of probability'. They mean the same. Sometimes the 'balance of probability' standard is expressed mathematically as '50 + % probability', but this can carry with it a danger of pseudo-mathematics, as the argument in this case demonstrated. When judging whether a case for believing that an event was caused in a particular way is stronger that the case for not so believing, the process is not scientific (although it may obviously include evaluation of scientific evidence) and to express the probability of some event having happened in percentage terms is illusory. ...

69. The judge's finding that the cause of the fire was 'very much less likely' to have been arcing of the Boa cable than the cigarette end discarded by Mr Nulty was reached after a painstaking examination of the evidence and was properly open to him. Rational analysis of the Boa cable theory showed that it was highly improbable. It would have required a remarkable combination of unlikely events. The objection to the discarded cigarette end theory was of a different nature. There was no comparable scientific or practical improbability about it. Mr Nulty was working alone at the relevant place and time. He had the opportunity and could well have had the temptation to do what the council alleged. The objection to it was that he would not have been expected to behave in such a way, but the circumstantial evidence that he did so on this occasion was compelling. In my view the judge was right to find that he did so and I would dismiss the appeal.

Are the judges able to rely upon statistical correlation?

Sienkiewicz v Greif (UK) Ltd [2011] 2 AC 229 Supreme Court

Lady Hale: ... **171.** The same applies to less sophisticated calculations. The fact that there are twice as many blue as yellow taxis about on the roads may double the risk that, if I am run over by a taxi, it will be by a blue rather than a yellow one. It may make it easier to predict that, if I am run over by a taxi, it will be by a blue rather than a yellow one. But when I am actually run over it does not prove that it was a blue taxi rather than a yellow taxi which was responsible. Likewise, if I actually develop breast cancer, the fact that there is a statistically significant relationship between, say, age at first child-bearing and developing the disease does not mean that that is what caused me to do so.

172. But as a fact finder, how can one ignore these statistical associations? Fact-finding judges are told that they must judge a conflict of oral evidence against 'the overall probabilities' coupled with the objective facts and contemporaneous documentation: see, for example, Robert Goff LJ in *Armagas Ltd v Mundogas SA (The 'Ocean Frost')* [1985] 1 Lloyd's Rep 1, 57. Millions of pounds may depend upon their decision. Yet judges do not define what they mean by 'the overall probabilities' other than their own particular hunches about human behaviour. Surely statistical associations are at least as valuable as hunches about human behaviour, especially when the judges are so unrepresentative of the population that their hunches may well be unreliable? Why should what a (always middle-aged and usually middle class and male) judge thinks probable in any given situation be thought more helpful than well-researched statistical associations in deciding where the overall probabilities lie? As it seems to me, both have a place. Finding facts is a difficult and under-studied exercise. But I would guess that it is not conducted on wholly scientific lines. Most judges will put everything into the mix before deciding which account is more likely than not. As long as they correctly direct themselves that statistical probabilities do not prove a case, any more than their own views about the overall probabilities will do so, their findings will be safe. ...

As Lady Hale says, finding facts is a difficult and under-researched exercise. The authority paradigm seems, however, to permit judges to have hunches. It would be idle to think that legal reasoning is a scientific exercise whatever the force of the authority paradigm.

FURTHER READING AND QUESTIONS

1. On the variety and complexities of reasoning within the common law tradition see generally Waddams (2003). The literature on legal causation is enormous and can be accessed via many of the latest editions of tort textbooks. For a comparison between legal reasoning in France and in the US see Lasser (2004).

2. 'When two opposite points of view are expressed with equal intensity, the truth does not necessarily lie exactly half way between. It is possible for one side simply to be wrong.' (Dawkins and Coyne). Can this assertion apply to legal argumentation?
3. 'Historians have noted that the shift from oral to written scripture often results in strident, misplaced certainty. Reading gives people the impression that they have an immediate grasp of their scripture; they are not compelled by a teacher to appreciate its complexity. Without the aesthetic and ethical disciplines of ritual, they can approach a text in a purely cerebral fashion, missing the emotive and therapeutic aspects of its stories and instructions' (Karen Armstrong). Does this observation offer any insights into legal thought and reasoning?
4. Imagine that a research student in a law faculty is drafting a research plan for a doctoral application or for a research grant. The research question is this. Does English law recognise a distinction between void and unenforceable contracts and, if so, what is the effect of such a distinction? There is a section on methodology that must be completed. Draft this section.
5. As above (question 4), but the research question is now this. Does English law recognise, and make use of, the concept of ownership?

6. The relationship between the official and unofficial portraits (2)

We have seen that despite the authority paradigm there are many opportunities in the reasoning process for judges to give expression to their own 'hunches', if not their own prejudices. The official portrait does not like to admit these opportunities – indeed the idea of judicial discretion is in the civil law systems something to be suppressed as much as possible – and a theorist like Ronald Dworkin has argued that the good judge does not use his or her discretion. But given the possibilities for 'hunches', what might a researcher operating under an inquiry paradigm make of legal reasoning?

6.1 INQUIRY PARADIGM AND SCHEMES OF INTELLIGIBILITY

Before one can tackle this question something first needs to be said about the inquiry paradigm.

> **Geoffrey Samuel, *An Introduction to Comparative Law Theory and Method*, Hart Publishing, 2014, pp 168–169** (footnotes omitted)
>
> A further paradigm dichotomy is one that might be expressed as that between the spirit of inquiry and the spirit of authority. It is concerned at one and the same time with the source of the knowledge in question, and with the spirit in which the object of knowledge is to be approached and understood. A spirit of *inquiry* is an orientation in which the motivating objective is to understand a phenomenon through a rigorous examination of all available physical evidence. This is the orientation which motivates research in the natural sciences where it has resulted in the Popper test. Any hypotheses emerging from research must be open to the test of falsification.
>
> In the social sciences, however, a hypothesis which does not meet this test may nonetheless be motivated by a spirit of inquiry. Indeed, in such disciplines as sociology, ethnology, demography and social psychology the sense of curiosity is surely the driving force. There is no epistemological free-for-all here. In both the natural and the social sciences the emphasis has been on methodology, that is to say on formalisation, quantification, control procedures

and demonstration. At this level, then, one can certainly talk in terms of normative restraint. But what is important is that these normative restraints, functioning at the methodological level, are themselves always open to debate and analysis. Nothing is out-of-bounds (so Popper, for example, has not been without his critics).

Recognising a distinction between the inquiry and authority paradigms is not to suggest that all doctrinal legal scholarship lacks completely a spirit of inquiry. The issue is one of epistemological scope and validity. In the natural sciences a hypothesis such as 'the dinosaurs were wiped out by a gigantic meteorite' is open to falsification. Someone might establish that this was not the cause of their disappearance. The objective facts will largely determine, in the end, the knowledge value of the hypothesis. Put another way, the hypothesis is validated by correspondence with an external object, which in turn will determine the 'truth' value of the hypothesis. It is either right or wrong.

There is, however, one science which cannot be validated by an external object, namely mathematics. Here, however, epistemological verification is determined by the internal coherence of mathematics rather than by correspondence. Three plus five has only one 'truth' answer and this is why mathematics is capable of being handled by a machine (calculator) (see 5.5). In contrast to the natural sciences, law has no external object as such and so an assertion by a judge is not open to falsification. Two contrasting answers to the same problem are perfectly acceptable.

***Transfield Shipping Inc v Mercator Shipping Inc* [2009] 1 AC 61**
House of Lords

Baroness Hale: **88.** Ship-owners let out their ship for a period of five to seven months, to end no later than midnight on 2 May 2004. The charterers notified the ship-owners that the ship would be back no later than then. The ship-owners therefore contracted to let the ship to new charterers for a period of about four to six months, promising that they could have the ship no later than 8 May 2004. The agreed price of hire was $39,500 a day. The ship was delayed on its last voyage and the owners did not get their ship back until 11 May 2004. The new charterers agreed to take the ship, but by then the market had fallen and they would only take it at a reduced price of $31,500 a day. Are the first charterers liable to pay only for the use of the ship for the number of days that they were late at the market rate then prevailing? Or are they liable to pay the difference between what the owners would have got from the new charter had the ship been returned in time and what the owners in fact got?

89. My Lords, this could be an examination question ... There is no obviously just answer: the charterer's default undoubtedly caused the owner's loss, but a loss for which no-one has ever had to pay before. The examiners would surely have given first class marks to all the judges who have answered the question so far. …

Some judges in this case thought that the profit could be recovered, other judges thought that it could not. But, says Baroness Hale, both assertions are capable of being 'right' (that is both are capable of obtaining first class marks).

What differentiates law from the natural sciences is a difference of scheme of intelligibility. As we shall see (in 6.2), scientists use a causal scheme to understand a phenomenon while a jurist often relies on a hermeneutical one. To assert that the dinosaurs were wiped out by a meteorite is to assert a causal explanation: phenomenon B was caused by phenomenon A. Whereas to assert that the shipowner's loss was within the 'contemplation' of the charterer at the time of the contract is to employ a hermeneutical approach: phenomenon B ('contemplation') signifies, or has a meaning which covers, phenomenon A (shipowner's loss).

These are not the only schemes. Six different ones were identified by a French social scientist epistemologist.

J-M Berthelot, Programmes, paradigmes, disciplines: pluralité et unité des sciences sociales, in J-M Berthelot (ed), *Épistémologie des sciences sociales*, Presses Universitaires de France, 2001, 457, p 484
(translation Geoffrey Samuel)

[T]he *causal* scheme (if x, then y or $y = f(x)$); the *functional* scheme (S→X→S, where one phenomenon X is analysed from the position of its function – X→S – in a given system); the *structural* scheme (where X results from a system founded, like language, on disjunctive rules, A or not A); the *hermeneutical* scheme (where X is the symptom, the expression of an underlying signification to be discovered through interpretation); the *actional* scheme (where X is the outcome, within a given space, of intentional actions); finally, the *dialectical* scheme (where X is the necessary outcome of the development of internal contradictions within a system).

The identification of these schemes of intelligibility marked a notable step forward in social science epistemology because it provided a framework for distinguishing not only the natural sciences from the social sciences and humanities, but also the plurality of approaches within the social sciences and humanities themselves.

6.2 EXPLANATION (CAUSATION) VERSUS MEANING (HERMENEUTICS)

So, why is legal reasoning different from reasoning in the natural sciences? Social science theorists have identified an important distinction between the sciences and the humanities. They have argued that the natural sciences are primarily concerned with *explaining* a phenomenon while the humanities are preoccupied with the *meaning* of a phenomenon.

Rudolf Makkreel, Expliquer et comprendre, in S Mesure and P Savidan (eds), *Le dictionnaire des sciences humaines*, Presses Universitaires de France, 2006, 441, p 441 (translation Geoffrey Samuel)

The distinction between explanation and understanding is as a general rule associated with the work of W Dilthey and refers to the fashion in which he opposed the sciences of nature and the human sciences. The natural sciences explain what is produced in nature while the human sciences offer elements of understanding of the processes of psychological and historical life. In fact JG Droysen introduced a similar distinction in order to distinguish history from the natural sciences. The distinction between explanation and understanding is based on the assertion of the deterministic character of explanations, whilst understanding involves a mode of intelligibility compatible with liberty. Because Droysen saw in history the sphere of human liberty, he estimated that it could not give rise to explanations. ...

The distinction has been contested by others, but it is useful to the extent that it identifies two different methodological schemes of intelligibility. This is the distinction between a causal scheme and a hermeneutical one.

Denis Thouard, Herméneutique, in S Mesure and P Savidan (eds), *Le dictionnaire des sciences humaines*, Presses Universitaires de France, 2006, 536, p 536 (translation Geoffrey Samuel)

Hermeneutics is first and foremost an art of interpretation. It appeared as a modern discipline in the 17th century attached to the elucidation of obscure but intelligible texts and discourses ... [H]ermeneutics ... is no longer concerned with the production of thoughts, that is the business of logic, but with the signification of the proffered discourse.

Hermeneutical activity is historically focused on three disciplines: 1/ *Theology*, where the interpretation is that of the Word of God ... which implies the absolute truth of what is to be interpreted and the perfection of the Author which is God; 2/ *Law*, where the interpretation of codes and statutes is undertaken not for itself or for a more profound understanding of the thoughts of the legislature, but for a particular case which raises nothing less than the constraining character of the legislative text; 3/ and finally the study of *secular texts* which offer a greater freedom since they are not inscribed in the same way in socially institutionalised functions, although the cultural, moral and atheistic values that they contain can be the object of a strong veneration.

It is important to note the distinction between production and signification. If one sees a road sign there are two broad knowledge questions that can be posed with respect to it. How did the sign come to be made and to be where it is? One is looking for an explanation of its physical existence and this question essentially brings into play a causal scheme of intelligibility. (One can also talk in terms of the production of a particular thought. How does one arrive at this particular mathematical result? This is a matter of logic.) The second question is about its signification. What does the sign mean? This question involves a hermeneutical scheme of intelligibility. As the above text indicates, lawyers spend their time explaining the meaning of legal texts (legislation, contracts, wills, cases and so on). Those working in the human and social sciences might also be applying a hermeneutical approach but equally there are those keen to explain social phenomena. Indeed perhaps meaning is explanation given the complexity of causes when it comes to examining the behaviour of humans. As a Nobel laureate once said: 'Think how hard physics would be if particles could think' (Murray Gell-Mann, quoted in Ariely, 2008, 244).

Take the causes of crime. What are they? What makes a question like this so difficult is that there is ambiguity and complexity at the level both of language and of fact. What does one mean by 'crime'? And what causes anti-social behaviour? Is the latter caused by individual moral (or lack of it) motivation (reasons), by social conditioning, by psychological orientation or what (causes)? Researchers disagree about this, in part because cause and reasoning become intertwined. If A shoots B dead the death of B has been caused by the bullet fired from the gun; but the reason why A shoots B is something different. In criminal law these two issues are distinguished in that there must be both *actus reus* (cause) and *mens rea* (reason), but they must be found together before a person can be convicted. In other words the mere act of, say, killing is not enough for a person to be convicted of murder; there must be an unlawful intention to kill. Equally an intention to kill is not sufficient; the intention must be accompanied by the act of killing. Sometimes the separation itself becomes the issue. A hits B intending to kill him and, some hours later, throws what he believes to be B's dead body into the river; in fact the blow did not kill B but the river subsequently did. Is A guilty of murder? Intention (reason) needs to be related to the events (cause) but this can only be done through an act of construction. Were there two events (blow and disposal) or just one event (series of acts as one event)? Meaning and explanation have become entangled.

6.3 INQUIRY PARADIGM AND HUMAN BEINGS

We have seen that physics would be hard if particles could think. Yet what if one has a human who cannot think? This can occur where a human loses the liberty of decision making. If one returns to the problem of crime, reasons and cause can become further intertwined in situations where the crime is dependent upon the absence of consent by the victim. A cuts into B with a knife; this will be both a crime and a civil wrong (tort of trespass) if B does not consent. However if A is a surgeon and B has consented to having the operation the position is transformed. Yet what if B is unconscious and cannot consent or refuse consent?

Airedale NHS Trust v Bland [1993] AC 789 House of Lords

This was an action for a declaration by a hospital authority that they could lawfully discontinue all life-sustaining treatment in respect of Anthony Bland, a victim of the Hillsborough football ground disaster. Bland was suffering a condition known as persistent vegetative state (PVS) from which, according to unanimous medical opinion, there could be no recovery. The parents and family supported the hospital's application. The House of Lords upheld an order of the first instance judge granting the declaration.

Lord Goff: ... I return to the patient who, because for example he is of unsound mind or has been rendered unconscious by accident or by illness, is incapable of stating whether or not he consents to treatment or care. In such circumstances, it is now established that a doctor may lawfully treat such a patient if he acts in his best interests, and indeed that, if the patient is already in his care, he is under a duty so to treat him: see *In re F. (Mental Patient: Sterilisation)* [1990] 2 AC 1, in which the legal principles governing treatment in such circumstances were stated by this House. For my part I can see no reason why, as a matter of principle, a decision by a doctor whether or not to initiate, or to continue to provide, treatment or care which could or might have the effect of prolonging such a patient's life, should not be governed by the same fundamental principle. ...

Lord Browne-Wilkinson: ... The answer to the question must of course depend on the circumstances of each case and there will be no single 'right' answer. Different doctors may take different views both on strictly medical issues and the broader ethical issues which the question raises. It follows that the legal question in this case (unlike the question which would arise if there were a parens patriae jurisdiction under which the court has to make the decision) is not whether the court thinks it is in the best interests of Anthony Bland to continue to receive intrusive medical care but whether the responsible doctor has reached a reasonable and bona fide belief that it is not ... Accordingly, on an application to the court for a declaration that the discontinuance of medical care will be lawful, the court's only concern will be to be satisfied that the doctor's decision to discontinue is in accordance with a respectable body of medical opinion and that it is reasonable.

'Best interests' in this context would seemingly be a question of fact (but note the interest model of reasoning: see 3.4). Yet surely this is a complete piece of fabrication by the two Law Lords? The authority paradigm can undoubtedly transform this notion of 'best interests' into a principle or at least a workable legal concept (see now Mental Capacity Act 2005 s 4). However, viewing it from the position of an inquiry paradigm the notion becomes a fiction as Lord Mustill seems to recognise. One is operating 'as if' the permanently unconscious person had 'best interests'.

Airedale NHS Trust v Bland [1993] AC 789 House of Lords

Lord Mustill: ... Threaded through the technical arguments addressed to the House were the strands of a much wider position, that it is in the best interests of the community at large that Anthony Bland's life should now end. The doctors have done all they can. Nothing will be gained by going on and much will be lost. The distress of the family will get steadily worse. The strain on the devotion of a medical staff charged with the care of a patient whose condition will never improve, who may live for years and who does not even recognise that he is being cared for, will continue to mount. The large resources of skill, labour and money now being devoted to Anthony Bland might in the opinion of many be more fruitfully employed in improving the condition of other patients, who if treated may have useful, healthy and enjoyable lives for years to come.

This argument was never squarely put, although hinted at from time to time. In social terms it has great force, and it will have to be faced in the end. But this is not a task which the courts can possibly undertake. A social cost-benefit analysis of this kind, which would have to embrace 'mercy killing' to which exactly the same considerations apply, must be for Parliament alone, and the outcome of it is at present quite impossible to foresee. Until the nettle is grasped, we must struggle on with the existing law, imperfect as it is. ...

I cannot accept this argument [based on *In re F*] which, if sound, would serve to legitimate a termination by much more direct means than are now contemplated. I can accept that a doctor in charge of a patient suffering the mental torture of Guillain-Barr syndrome, rational but trapped and mute in an unresponsive body, could well feel it imperative that a decision on whether to terminate life could wait no longer and that the only possible decision in the interests of the patient, even leaving out all the other interests involved, would be to end it here and now by a speedy and painless injection. Such a conclusion would attract much sympathy, but no doctrine of best interests could bring it within the law.

> Quite apart from this the case of Anthony Bland seems to me quite different. He feels no pain and suffers no mental anguish. Stress was laid in argument on the damage to his personal dignity by the continuation of the present medical regime, and on the progressive erosion of the family's happy recollections by month after month of distressing and hopeless care. Considerations of this kind will no doubt carry great weight when Parliament comes to consider the whole question in the round. But it seems to me to be stretching the concept of personal rights beyond breaking point to say that Anthony Bland has an interest in ending these sources of others' distress. Unlike the conscious patient he does not know what is happening to his body, and cannot be affronted by it; he does not know of his family's continuing sorrow. By ending his life the doctors will not relieve him of a burden become intolerable, for others carry the burden and he has none. What other considerations could make it better for him to die now rather than later? None that we can measure, for of death we know nothing. The distressing truth which must not be shirked is that the proposed conduct is not in the best interests of Anthony Bland, for he has no best interests of any kind.

One difficulty with this problem of the permanently unconscious patient is that in allowing him to die one is in breach of his human right to life. How can it be in his 'best interest' to violate a fundamental right? This is not necessarily to criticise the actual decision. The point to be made is that legal reasoning is not really able to deal with this kind of issue in any convincing way because it is trapped within its own conceptual thinking. One gets close to treating the human as a piece of inert property.

> ***In re S (Hospital Patient: Court's Jurisdiction)*** **[1995] 3 WLR 78**
> **Court of Appeal**
>
> **Millett LJ**: This is not a case about medical treatment or the withdrawal of medical treatment, nor is it a case about the provision or withdrawal of care. It is in effect a custody dispute between two parties each of whom claims the right to look after an elderly gentleman (whom I will call 'the patient') in accordance with what each of them plausibly asserts he would wish if he were not by reason of incapacity unable to formulate or communicate his wishes. ...
>
> If the patient were a sack of potatoes, instead of a living person unable by reason of incapacity of making his wishes known, the court would have undoubted jurisdiction to resolve any dispute between rival claimants. It would do so by resort to considerations of legal title and possession. Why should it make a difference that the subject matter of the dispute is the right to look after a human being, and that the resolution of the dispute depends upon ascertaining his wishes or, if they cannot be ascertained, by determining what is in his best interest and inferring that that is what he would wish?

A person cannot of course openly be treated as a sack of potatoes (although legal systems have considered people as property rather than humans or full humans), but Tony Bland was effectively being treated as a *res* and humanised only through the attribution of having 'interests'. But, as Lord Mustill noted, was it really his interest that was in play or those of others? The irony of legal reasoning, when compared to reasoning in the physical sciences, is that liberty of action is fundamental and is built into the whole conceptual structure. Intention and consent are everywhere in the law. What causes problems is when the human loses this power of liberty and effectively is being transferred from the law of persons to the law of things. Yet perhaps all legal reasoning is about reducing everything to a matter of material 'interests'?

6.4 LEVEL OF OBSERVATION

Another fundamental knowledge point made by sociologists is that when the level of observation changes the knowledge changes.

Dominique Desjeux, *Les sciences sociales*, Presses Universitaires de France, 2004, p 5, 95 (translation Geoffrey Samuel)

The point to be made at the outset is that, according to the focal point or level of observation chosen, observed reality changes, the points of reference are transformed, the rationality question evolves and the variables which seem independent to an economist can become dependent for a psychologist at her level of observation and *vice versa*.

It is, then, a method which arises out of methodological relativism. The results obtained in an investigation depend on the position of the observer, the observation conditions, the level of the observation and how reality is divided up at any given level. According to the viewpoints, the points of reference, the form of the phenomena, the methods and therefore the description of reality can all change. ...

... [I]t is not because I work as a historian on the long view that there are not individual heroes or great men. If I focus on the individual at the micro-individual level, from a psychological or sociological point of view, it is normal not to see social classes or institutions, but I cannot say that they do not exist. At best I can say that it is a subject that does not interest me or which does not appear central in relation to the problem that I am researching. ...

The level of observation is relevant to legal reasoning because it can determine how facts are perceived. A ship sinks taking with it the passengers and crew: do they all die at the same time or do they perish at different times? This can be vital when it comes to interpreting a document such as a will: see *Re Rowland* (above 4.4). The same is true with regard to events, already discussed, such as the hitting of a victim with an intention to kill and the subsequent disposal of the victim without such an intention. Is this two separate events or just one?

6.5 ACTIONALISM AND METHODOLOGICAL INDIVIDUALISM

The level of observation reflects itself, to some extent at least, within the various schemes of intelligibility. Structuralism and systems tend to suggest a somewhat holistic vision of a phenomenon, especially when applied to social objects such as societies. And certainly the institutional plan or system presents a cohesive and seemingly holistic view of law. However on closer inspection the institutional system is focused on individual persons and individual things and the relations between them. It is, in its essence, a model consisting of individual people (actors) who own or possess individualised things and who contract with other individuals. Of course many 'persons' turn out to be legal persons (corporations) which are evidently a group phenomenon; but the assumption made by the law, as we have seen (see 4.6), is that these corporations are individuals. This individualism is important in legal reasoning.

Read v J Lyons & Co [1945] 1 KB 216 Court of Appeal

Scott LJ: ... [O]ur law of torts is concerned not with activities but with acts. ...

With the rise of industry and motor vehicles the number of accidents involving death and personal injury rose sharply. Yet the number of people killed and injured on the roads and in the workplace each year is statistically predictable (with some ups and downs), which suggests that there is a defined human cost attaching to such an activity. However, English law does not look at work or traffic accidents in this way; it treats each car accident as resulting from the act of an individual which can be assessed in terms of individual fault or its absence (*Mansfield v Weetabix Ltd* [1998] 1 WLR 1263). Such an approach was also to be found in *Tesco v Nattrass* (see 4.6). How different the foundation of liability might be if the law of tort saw personal injury as resulting from activities rather than acts.

Jacques Moreau, *La responsabilité administrative*, Presses Universitaires de France, 1986, p 110 (translation Geoffrey Samuel)

In the three cases just cited, the justification of liability without fault is rather that a certain equilibrium has been broken – and must be re-established by the award of damages – between, on the one hand, a behaviour of the administration that is taken to be inspired by the general interest aim (it is, among other things a part of the definition of the notion of public works) and which 'benefits everyone' and, on the other hand, a 'burden', a relatively serious injury which falls only upon certain persons (adjoining owners, those who assist the administration, public officials exposed to risk, those destined to be affected by certain administrative regulations). The sought after basis of liability is, then, *the equality of citizens before public burdens*, as the frequent conclusions of the *commissaires de gouvernement* and the judgments of certain cases indicate more and more clearly. ...

This French principle of equality is founded on a much more holistic vision of society. In English law the emphasis is traditionally on the individual, which generates a very different vision of liability.

***Dunne v North Western Gas Board* [1964] 2 QB 806 Court of Appeal**

Sellers LJ: ... Gas, water and also electricity services are well-nigh a necessity of modern life, or at least are generally demanded as a requirement for the common good, and one or more are being taken with considerable despatch to every village and hamlet in the country with either statutory compulsion or sanction. It would seem odd that facilities so much sought after by the community and approved by their legislators should be actionable at common law because they have been brought to places where they are required and have escaped without negligence by an unforeseen sequence of mishaps. A sequence of events may be just as unforeseeable and unavoidable and as extraneous to an individual or a supplier of services as an act of God is recognised to be. ...

An act of God would seem to take precedence over equality and the sharing of burdens. However a more recent case has seemingly shifted the emphasis a little way towards the French approach.

***Dennis v Ministry of Defence* [2003] EWHC 793 Queen's Bench Division**

Buckley J: **1.** This case concerns the effect of noise from Harrier jet fighters on the 1st Claimant's neighbouring estate. It is alleged to constitute a nuisance at common law and/or to infringe his human rights, and also to infringe the human rights of his wife, the 2nd Claimant. A declaration and damages are sought, alternatively damages of some £10,000,000. ...

46. The problem with putting the public interest into the scales when deciding whether a nuisance exists, is simply that if the answer is no, not because the claimant is being over sensitive, but because his private rights must be subjugated to the public interest, it might well be unjust that he should suffer the damage for the benefit of all. If it is to be held that there is no nuisance, there can be no remedy at common law. As this case illustrates, the greater the public interest, the greater may be the interference. If public interest is considered at the remedy stage and since the court has a discretion, the nuisance may continue but the public, in one way or another, pays for its own benefit ... Allowing a human rights claim but denying a remedy in nuisance would, of course, be another solution, but it would be one that reflected adversely on the flexibility of the common law. ...

47. The principles or policy underlying these considerations are that public interest should be considered and that selected individuals should not bear the cost of the public benefit. I am in favour of giving effect to those principles. I believe it is necessary to do so if the common law in this area is to be consistent with the developing jurisprudence on human rights.

Whether this approach will ultimately be approved by a superior court is an interesting question. It certainly displays a less individualistic outlook. Public benefit proves to be the key notion in this liability question. If one takes a strictly individualistic viewpoint then the public as individuals should be glad of a public service and take the risk, as individuals, if things associated with the activity of supply go wrong. If one looks at public benefit as benefitting the public as a group, then the position changes; it seemingly becomes unjust that an individual should be burdened with the risk of the activity that benefits the group.

Is this difference of view one that can be reduced to politics? It was a right-wing politician who asserted that 'there is no such thing as society'. There are 'only individual men and women and there are families' (M Thatcher, *Woman's Own*, 31 October 1987). More left-leaning judges might be tempted to assert that there is such a thing as society and that there are general interests that attach to it. An 'actional' scheme of intelligibility – that is one that sees human society only as a mass of individual actors – is no doubt a fundamental epistemological position in social science research. But it is also an ideological one.

This said, there are methodological problems that attach to a holistic approach, at least with regard to social science methods.

Sienkiewicz v Greif (UK) Ltd **[2011] 2 AC 229 Supreme Court**

Lord Dyson: ... **218.** ... It is often the basic impossibility of proving individual causation which distinguishes toxic tort cases from ordinary personal injury cases. As Mr Gold [(1986) 96 Yale LJ 376] points out, epidemiology is based on

> the study of populations, not individuals. It seeks to establish associations between alleged causes and effects. With proper scientific interpretation, these correlations lend great weight to an inference of causation. However, in an individual case, epidemiology alone cannot *conclusively* prove causation. At best, it can establish only a certain probability that a randomly selected case of disease was one that would not have occurred absent exposure. ...

A statistical correlation between, say, the class of person who goes to university is useful information; but such information does not *explain* why people of a certain class do not tend to go to university. One needs to do research at the level of individual families to obtain this knowledge. In other words an actional scheme has its role within the inquiry paradigm.

6.6 STRUCTURALISM VERSUS HERMENEUTICS (RECEPTION THEORY)

We have already seen that a hermeneutical scheme of intelligibility puts the emphasis on meaning (see 6.2). But where should the emphasis be placed when it comes to determining this meaning? This is a question that has arisen in literary and cinema studies under a broad heading entitled 'reception theory'.

> **Chris Dzialo, Reception Theory, in E Branigan and W Buckland (eds), *The Routledge Encyclopedia of Film Theory*, Routledge, 2014, 390, p 390**
>
> 'Reception theory' refers both to a model for literary history developed by Hans Robert Jauss in 1967 and to a more general approach in literary and film and media studies. In its recent incarnation, reception theory does not denote a theory *per se* but rather a collection of models, practices, and heuristics that are concerned with historicized and active responses by readers and viewers as opposed to intended meanings by authors and film-makers. ...

One of the more sophisticated versions of this theory or approach is to be found in the work of Janet Staiger.

> **Chris Dzialo, Reception Theory, in E Branigan and W Buckland (eds), *The Routledge Encyclopedia of Film Theory*, Routledge, 2014, 390, p 392**
>
> Staiger's reception project begins with *Interpreting Films: Studies in the Historical Reception of American Cinema* (1992). Here she demarcates the landscape of literary theory into three categories: 'text-activated', 'reader activated', and

'context-activated theories' (Staiger, 1992, 34–48). 'Text-activated theories' are those positing a strong text that determines the meaning for the reader – envisioned as a more or less passive participant in the process. Structuralism and formalism are examples of text-activated theories for Staiger. On the flip side of the coin, 'reader-activated theories' are those that posit a weak text and a strong reader. Here, a reader's personal experiences and psychology explain the meaning of a text better than any intended meaning by an author; ...

... 'Context-activated theories' are a middle-ground of sorts concerned with the historical and social contexts surrounding the process of reading. These theories posit that meaning arises from the interplay between a reader, the text, and surrounding historical and social forces. ...

It has already been seen that film theory can be relevant for lawyers, especially with regard to the use of images in legal reasoning and with regard to the notion of *persona* (see 4.6). Here film theory is offering a different insight. It is indicating how a hermeneutical approach is not just a matter of interpretation but a kind of relation with the text in which both the author and the reader interact within a historical and a social context. Given the central role of texts in law and legal reasoning, reception theory clearly has relevance. Indeed the extract from Lady Hale in the *Woodland* case is a good example of a judge placing emphasis more on a 'reader-activated' approach than a 'text-activated' one (see 4.8).

***White (Frost) v Chief Constable of South Yorkshire* [1999] 2 AC 455 House of Lords**

Lord Steyn: ... Moreover, as the majority in the Court of Appeal was uncomfortably aware, the awarding of damages to these police officers sits uneasily with the denial of the claims of bereaved relatives by the decision of the House of Lords in *Alcock*. The decision of the Court of Appeal has introduced an imbalance in the law of tort which might perplex the man on the Underground. ...

This was the approach that stimulated Lady Hale into adopting her reasoning in *Woodland*. But other examples of what might be called 'reader-activated' are to be found in cases where judges refer to fictional individuals such as the 'reasonable person' or 'commercial person'.

***Mannai Investment Co v Eagle Star Life Assurance* [1997] AC 749 House of Lords**

Lord Hoffmann: ... In the case of commercial contracts, the restriction on the use of background has been quietly dropped. There are certain special kinds of evidence, such as previous negotiations and express declarations of intent, which for practical reasons which it is unnecessary to analyse, are inadmissible in aid of construction. They can be used only in an action for rectification. But apart from these exceptions, commercial contracts are construed in the light of all the background which could reasonably have been expected to have been available to the parties in order to ascertain what would objectively have been understood to be their intention: *Prenn v Simmonds* [1971] 1 WLR 1381, 1383. The fact that the words are capable of a literal application is no obstacle to evidence which demonstrates what a reasonable person with knowledge of the background would have understood the parties to mean, even if this compels one to say that they used the wrong words. In this area, we no longer confuse the meaning of words with the question of what meaning the use of the words was intended to convey. ...

Lord Steyn: ... In determining the meaning of the language of a commercial contract, and unilateral contractual notices, the law ... generally favours a commercially sensible construction. The reason for this approach is that a commercial construction is more likely to give effect to the intention of the parties. Words are therefore interpreted in the way in which a reasonable commercial person would construe them. And the standard of the reasonable commercial person is hostile to technical interpretations and undue emphasis on niceties of language. ...

Accordingly it is possible to conclude that, at least in regard to the interpretation of contracts, there is a movement away from a 'text-activated theory' towards a 'context-activated' theory.

***Investors Compensation Scheme v West Bromwich Building Society* [1998] 1 WLR 896 House of Lords**

Lord Hoffmann: ... Interpretation is the ascertainment of the meaning which the document would convey to a reasonable person having all the background knowledge which would reasonably have been available to the parties in the situation in which they were at the time of the contract.

Value judgements on the part of the reader may equally be important in determining a decision. In this situation the decision-maker might depart from a previous text (or policy rule) on the basis that the context has changed.

***Michael v Chief Constable of South Wales Police* [2015] UKSC 2 Supreme Court**

Lord Kerr (dissenting): ... **161.** ... A decision based on what is considered to be correct legal principle cannot be lightly set aside in subsequent cases where the same legal principle is in play. By contrast, a decision which is not the product of, in the words of Lord Oliver, 'any logical process of analogical deduction' holds less sway, particularly if it does not accord with what the subsequent decision-maker considers to be the correct instinctive reaction to contemporaneous standards and conditions. Put bluntly, what one group of judges felt was the correct policy answer in 2009, should not bind another group of judges, even as little as five years later. ...

A more general reception theory approach might be found with respect to the problem of exclusion clauses in contract. The original rule was clear enough:

***Printing and Numerical Registering Co v Sampson* (1875) LR 19 Eq 462**
Chancery Division

Sir George Jessel: ... If there is one thing more than another which public policy requires, it is that men of full age and competent understanding shall have the utmost liberty of contracting and that their contracts, when entered into freely and voluntarily, shall be held sacred and shall be enforced by courts of justice. ...

However the reception of this rule was modified over the next century:

***George Mitchell (Chesterhall) Ltd v Finney Lock Seeds Ltd* [1983] QB 284**
Court of Appeal

Lord Denning MR: ... None of you nowadays will remember the trouble we had – when I was called to the Bar – with exemption clauses. They were printed in small print on the back of tickets and order forms and invoices. They were contained in catalogues or timetables. They were held to be binding on any person who took them without objection. No one ever did object. He never read them or knew what was in them. No matter how unreasonable they were, he was bound. All this was done in the name of 'freedom of contract.' But the freedom was all on the side of the big concern which had the use of the printing press. No freedom for the little man who took the ticket or order form or invoice. The big concern said, 'Take it or leave it.' The little man had no option but to take it. The big concern could and did exempt itself from liability in its own interest without regard to the little man. It got away with it time after time. When the courts said to the big concern, 'You must put it in clear words,' the big concern had no hesitation in doing so. It knew well that the little man would never read the exemption clauses or understand them. ...

Faced with this abuse of power – by the strong against the weak – by the use of the small print of the conditions – the judges did what they could to put a curb upon it. They still had before them the idol, 'freedom of contract.' They still knelt down and worshipped it, but they concealed under their cloaks a secret weapon. They used it to stab the idol in the back. This weapon was called 'the true construction of the contract.' They used it with great skill and ingenuity. They used it so as to depart from the natural meaning of the words of the exemption clause and to put upon them a strained and unnatural construction. In case after case, they said that the words were not strong enough to give the big concern exemption from liability; or that in the circumstances the big concern was not entitled to rely on the exemption clause. If a ship deviated from the contractual voyage, the owner could not rely on the exemption clause. If a warehouseman stored the goods in the wrong warehouse, he could not pray in aid the limitation clause. If the seller supplied goods different in kind from those contracted for, he could not rely on any exemption from liability. If a shipowner delivered goods to a person without production of the bill of lading, he could not escape responsibility by reference to an exemption clause. In short, whenever the wide words – in their natural meaning – would give rise to an unreasonable result, the judges either rejected them as repugnant to the main purpose of the contract, or else cut them down to size in order to produce a reasonable result ... But when the clause was itself reasonable and gave rise to a reasonable result, the judges upheld it; at any rate, when the clause did not exclude liability entirely but only limited it to a reasonable amount. So where goods were deposited in a cloakroom or sent to a laundry for cleaning, it was quite reasonable for the company to limit their liability to a reasonable amount, having regard to the small charge made for the service. ...

In many ways this move away from 'text-activated' approaches towards more functionalist (or more 'contextual-activated') schemes is, or was, also represented by the shift away from structuralist and formalist theories of law (see 5.5).

Lister v Hesley Hall Ltd [2002] 1 AC 215 House of Lords

Lord Steyn: ... **16.** ... A preoccupation with conceptualistic reasoning may lead to the absurd conclusion that there can only be vicarious liability if the bank carries on business in defrauding its customers. Ideas divorced from reality have never held much attraction for judges steeped in the tradition that their task is to deliver principled but practical justice. How the courts set the law on a sensible course is a matter to which I now turn. ...

In the civil law tradition – where private law is based on statutory codes – reception theory could be said to have had a fundamental role.

Leone Niglia, _The Struggle for European Private Law: A Critique of Codification_, Hart Publishing, 2015, p 157

I have explained that codification is a dynamic and never-static phenomenon, for, to exaggerate, there is never a well-defined code-text, but always interpretation of it and perspectives on it – and struggles. Understanding a code is about

> capturing these perspectives, and capturing them is about detecting struggles as well as participating in them … A code, once enacted, may enjoy weak authority or no authority at all in being highly contested and resisted, depending on the degrees of contestation and resistance that surround the code-product. …

Professor Niglia is here echoing a phenomenon that a film theorist, by analogy, would regard as an example of reception theory. The legislator who produces a code no doubt hopes that it will be 'text-activated' and as soon as there is a movement away from the text towards a 'reader-activated' approach one might regard the code – as Napoléon apparently did about his *Code civil* – as being lost ('*Mon Code est perdu*').

6.7 POSTMODERN AND POST-AXIOMATIC APPROACHES

Another contribution that literary and cinema studies have made to theory is the use of the notion of postmodernism. As a theoretical concept or category it tends to be rather weak and certainly is of little epistemological (knowledge) value in itself. Yet it can express, in a very general way, certain trends and themes of the latter part of the 20th century. One theme is the idea of a post-axiomatic era that perhaps starts with American Realism. However, to understand this idea of a 'post-axiomatic' period one must first put it into an epistemological context. Writing about the history of the sciences, one philosopher has identified a number of epistemological stages.

> **Robert Blanché, *L'épistémologie*, Presses Universitaires de France, 3rd ed, 1983, p 65** (translation Geoffrey Samuel)
>
> … Rather than a binary division [between concrete and abstract science] it is necessary to deal here with a continuous development. One should speak more of the distinction between deductive science and inductive science. Mathematics started out by being inductive, and the sciences said to be inductive often take, and always aspire to take, the deductive form. Deduction and induction mark two stages in the development of science, the stages themselves being framed within an initial stage and a final stage. In fact it appears that all the sciences follow, in distinguishing themselves only by their degree of advancement, a similar course, passing or being called to pass, successively through the descriptive, inductive, deductive and axiomatic stages.

These stages certainly seem relevant for law. Early Roman legal thought might well be described as descriptive while that of the Classical period and, much later, the medieval era can be seen as inductive; the Humanists triggered a move from the inductive stage to the deductive while the 19th-century German Pandectists took thinking into the axiomatic (see generally Stein, 1999; Gordley, 2013). The problem now is, as James Gordley puts it, *Ubinam Gentium Sumus* (Where in the world are we)?

James Gordley, *The Jurists: A Critical History*, Oxford University Press, 2013, p 277 (footnotes omitted)

In the twentieth century, the attack on deductive logic and on the elucidation of concepts without regard to purpose was pressed in the United States, by Roscoe Pound and by the American legal realists; in France, it was taken up by Bonnecase; in Germany, by the *Freijuristen*, the school of *Interessenjurisprudenz*, and the advocates of 'legal sociology.'

Although there was general agreement on what legal concepts are not and on how they should not be used, there was less on what they are and how they might be. To resolve that question, the critics would have had to rethink epistemological and metaphysical problems inherited from the rationalists. That would have been difficult.

One can say at a very general level that we are in a 'post-axiomatic' world. The difficulty is that while one can see the frame one cannot see very clearly the contents (to use a metaphor from the mouth of the main character in Jacques Tourneur's magnificent *Out of the Past* (1947)). What is the methodological and epistemological basis of this 'post-axiomatic' period? Some, as Steve Hedley has trenchantly observed, are urging a return to the 'axiomatic' or formalist period.

Steve Hedley, Looking Outward or Looking Inward? Obligations Scholarship in the Early 21st Century, in Andrew Robertson and Tang Hang Wu (eds), *The Goals of Private Law*, Hart, 2009, p 199
(footnotes omitted)

When it comes to a detailed statement of the law of obligations, it is striking how much of the modern vision of the internalists [those looking at law from an internal point of view] merely repeats the views of leading law teachers circa 1880. Those who look inward see an antique set of rules. Certainly contract has changed very little: a modern teacher who reads the first editions of Pollock or Anson on contract will find little that is strange. The tort books of that time would be a little stranger, no doubt, though mostly on matters of emphasis rather than substance. Restitution is the newest component of obligations, though its writers have rapidly 'traditionalised' themselves by the rapid ingestion of large slabs of

> Romanist thought. Crucially, the underlying political assumptions of the Victorian text writers and the modern internalists would apparently be the same: namely that the topic under discussion is justice between individuals, not wider concerns of social justice; … And where the internalists appear to have innovated, it is usually simply by completing projects that the Victorians themselves started but left incomplete: finding a unitary basis for tort, or finding a more satisfactory description of the materials traditionally labelled 'quasi-contract'.
>
> We are so used to this that it has ceased to strike us as odd. But it is odd. Every other branch of human knowledge – including legal knowledge – has progressed immeasurably over the past century. In any other area, academics would be embarrassed at using much the same theories and attitudes as were advanced a century and a half ago, with nothing to show for the work of the intervening period except some minor updating. …

One way of describing the 'post-axiomatic' is, then, to deny the 'post' part and return judging and reasoning to an 'axiomatic' method founded upon a highly formalised conceptual structure of rights and (or) duties completely isolated from social (instrumental) goals. Structuralism should trump functionalism. But is a return to such axiomatic or formalist thinking a realistic proposition? As Gordley says, such legal thinking came in for a sustained attack and while realism itself has been criticised by the neo-formalists it is difficult to imagine that common law judges are going to abandon remedies, policy and interest reasoning in favour of a rigid 'top-down' approach (see 5.1). That has never been part of the English common law methodology with its tradition of individual judgments. Indeed it is difficult to imagine the civil law world succumbing once again to the kind of abstract conceptual thinking that dominated the 19th century.

If one returns to the somewhat vague category of 'postmodern' thinking, film studies might offer a further critical insight into the current re-emphasis on formalist thinking.

> **Catherine Constable, Postmodern Cinema, in E Branigan and W Buckland (eds), *The Routledge Encyclopedia of Film Theory*, Routledge, 2014, 376, pp 378, 379**
>
> Jameson argues that the rise of pastiche marks the end of the modernist author, the individual genius who generates his or her 'own unique vision of the world and … own unique, unmistakable style' (114). … Jameson consistently conceptualizes pastiche as a practice that marks the end of Romantic conceptions of authorship. Pastiche occurs 'in a world in which stylistic innovation is no longer possible, [where] all that is left is to imitate dead styles' (115) … [T]he phrase 'postmodern auteur' is a contradiction in terms. …

> ... Thus the evocation of a non-specific past is a move beyond history that collapses the timeline of past to present, ultimately leaving us unable to understand the past or conceptualize our own present. ...

Of course films are a very different phenomenon than law. But one wonders if some of the criticism aimed at postmodern cinema might by analogy be transferable to the legal field. Steve Hedley's criticism of the contemporary 'internalist' theorists read a little like Fredric Jameson's criticism of postmodern pastiche. Is not the return to formalism equally signalling a collapse of the timeline between past and present in legal thinking? Does not such formalism leave the contemporary jurist unable to understand the past or to conceptualise the present?

6.8 LAW AS FICTION (FICTION THEORY)

Cinema, like literature, is closely associated with fiction and, as such, fiction as a concept would at first sight seem to be quite far removed from the discipline of law. However the notion of 'fiction' is to be found in law in as much as legal fictions – one of which is (in English law) the legal person (see 4.8) – is an important topic that has attracted its own legal literature. Indeed fictions in law are not just a topic in their own right; fiction theory is still capable of exercising considerable force – and not just in law.

> **JW Jones, *Historical Introduction to the Theory of Law*, Oxford University Press, 1940, pp 165–166** (footnotes omitted)
>
> *The philosophy of 'as if'.* To the world at large the legal fiction has always provided the most characteristic example of the mental processes which are regarded as peculiar to lawyers ... Therefore it is somewhat gratifying to the self-esteem of lawyers that in the hands of Vaihinger the legal fiction has become the starting-point of a new system of philosophy. Instead of being an odd anomaly, it takes its place as the type of a mental process which is indispensable if thinking of any sort is possible. The human mind, says the philosophy of 'as if', is so constituted that it cannot dispense with fictions. There can be no thought without abstract concepts and these concepts are nothing more than fictions. ...

The point must be stressed that fiction theory as developed by Hans Vaihinger (1852–1933) in his work *Die Philosophie des Als Ob* (1911), is more subtle than it might first appear. Indeed it ties in with representation theory, which we looked at earlier (see 4.8) where Henry Bacon noted that we 'assume material reality exists irrespective of our consciousness but only representations enable us to create a meaningful and workable relationship to that reality.' These 'representations' are, for Vaihinger, fictions in the sense that they are models of 'reality' whose value can only be judged in terms of their pragmatic usefulness. Hans Vaihinger is thus more of an epistemologist than a philosopher. He is more interested in a theory of knowledge representation.

Christophe Bouriau, *Le 'comme si': Kant, Vaihinger et le fictionalisme*, Éditions du Cerf, 2013, p 119 (translation Geoffrey Samuel)

The philosophy of 'acting as if' refers primarily to a certain epistemological attitude. 'To act as if' such and such idea was true is opposed to the assertion that this idea is actually true. In saying: 'act *as if* these ideas were true, we reject any pronouncement on their truth or false value to concentrate instead on their theoretical or practical usefulness. For example, in saying 'Let us reason as if matter is made up of atoms', the academic avoids, according to Vaihinger, the endless ontological debates of this kind – 'Is material actually made up of atoms?' – to focus instead on the fruitfulness of the atomistic model.

Should lawyers take Hans Vaihinger seriously? Certainly one of the most important legal theorists of the 20th century, Hans Kelsen, came to the conclusion, after studying Vaihinger, that his own legal theory was ultimately founded upon a fiction (the *Grundnorm*).

Christophe Bouriau, *Les fictions du droit : Kelsen, lecteur de Vaihinger*, ENS Éditions, p 31 (translation Geoffrey Samuel)

... Provided that an unverifiable idea be empirically useful to science, let us not make claims about its hypothetical value and let us be content to accord it a fictional status.

Kelsen insisted many times on this last point with respect to his 'fundamental norm': it was a supposition, and nothing more than that, without any pretention to reflect reality. It is not therefore relevant to reject it on the ground that it does not exist or that it does not satisfy the factual conditions to be admitted as a norm: 'It is not a positive norm, that is to say one posed by a real act of the will, but a presupposed norm in legal thought, that is to say (as has been shown earlier on) a fictional norm'. ...

And if one returns to the level of legal reasoning and concepts one fundamental fiction, in addition to legal personality, is adoption. An adopted child is treated 'as if' it is the natural child of the adopting couple. In Roman law this adopted child fiction was often expressed through the use of the Latin term *quasi* and what is important about this term is that it was employed quite regularly by the Roman jurists.

> **Digest of Justinian, Book 15, Title 3** (translation Geoffrey Samuel)
>
> 1. ULPIAN, *On the Edict, Book 29.* If those in the power of another have nothing in their *peculium*, or not enough to cover what is owed, those who have them in their power are held liable if they have materially benefitted from the transaction: it is, seemingly, as if he [the master] had himself contracted (*quasi cum ipsis potius contractum videatur*).

What is interesting about this text is that it shows how 'as if' fiction theory can be useful in the understanding of legal reasoning. Some situations are so close to contract that they should be treated 'as if' a party had actually contracted. Indeed the Romans finally invented a whole 'quasi' category to house these 'as if' contracts and 'as if' delicts. These two quasi categories have, however, come in for a sustained attack.

> **Peter Birks, Definition and Division: A Meditation on *Institutes* 3.13, in P Birks (ed), *The Classification of Obligations*, Oxford University Press, 1997, pp 18–19**
>
> The fourfold classification which stands in Justinian's *Institutes* is a response to the challenge of the residual miscellany. It accepts Gaius's two main causative events, contract and wrong, and then it purports to resolve the miscellany by recognising that other obligations arise either as though from a contract or as though from a wrong, a statement which all too easily metamorphoses into the rather different affirmation that they arise either from a quasi-contract or a quasi-wrong. Beauty is not always the ally of truth. The elegant symmetry deceives. For this is only a variation upon the theme that all birds must be either pigeons or sparrows. It merely says that all those which are neither pigeons nor sparrows must be counted either as though they were pigeons or as though they were sparrows. In effect, therefore, the *quasi* categories left the challenge of resolving the miscellany unconquered, though the almost scriptural authority long enjoyed by the Roman law library made it difficult to mount effective attacks upon the pseudo-resolution sanctioned by Justinian.

This attack by the late Professor Birks on the two categories is misleading in a number of ways. First, it is an epistemological error to consider taxonomy in zoology as being the same as taxonomy in law; the two schemes are quite different. Classification in the natural sciences is about categorising external objects whereas classification in law is not. One classifies in zoology according to criteria that are as much stimulated by these external objects as by the science of zoology itself. In law the categories are constructed entirely by the discourse of law itself and legal texts and cases are then arranged according to this constructed scheme (see Samuel, 2000 and 2004).

Secondly, the pigeons and sparrows analogy misunderstands the basis of the quasi categories as developed within Roman legal reasoning. As we have said, some situations are so close to contract that it seemed reasonable to the Roman jurists to treat them 'as if' there existed a contract. These 'as if' situations, which were relatively few in number, were not really residual miscellany; they were attached in terms of their factual situations to factual situations that were categorised as contract and wrongs.

Thirdly, even if the quasi categories are fictitious in the 'as if' sense, the same could be said of all legal categories. Professor Birks argued that contract and wrongs (delicts) were responses to 'causative events', but these causative events are no less fictional, given the sheer complexity of causation, than the quasi categories. 'In retaining one cause', writes Christophe Bouriau in his work on Vaihinger, 'we abusively simplify the complexity of what is real' (Bouriau, 2013, 110). 'Contracts' and 'wrongs' do not exist empirically; parties act 'as if' there is a binding contract which gives rise to an obligation to perform or to liability in contract. And courts impose liability in delict 'as if' there has been fault which has caused the damage. What is meant here is not that there is an absence of agreement or negligence as such; they are just models of liability which require that agreement or fault be proved in court on the balance of probabilities. Some cases bring out this 'as if' nature of the exercise better than others (see eg *Milton Keynes BG v Nulty*, above 5.7).

From the point of view of fiction theory, what matters, then, is the usefulness of the legal concepts and categories that act as the foundation for a reasoning model. One tests the different reasoning models not on the basis of whether 'rights', 'interests', 'policy' and so on actually represent some empirical truth, but on the basis of whether they generate rational results 'as if' they existed. To quote, once again, the film theorist Henry Bacon: we 'assume material reality exists irrespective of our consciousness but only representations enable us to create a meaningful and workable relationship to that reality'.

FURTHER READING AND QUESTIONS

1. On schemes of intelligibility see Samuel (2014, 81–92) and on reception theory see Staiger (1992). With regard to fiction theory, see Del Mar and Twining (2015). Legal taxonomy is examined in further depth in Samuel (2000), (2004) and (2005).
2. How different would legal reasoning in the law of tort be if our law of tort was 'concerned with activities rather than acts'?
3. Could the case of *Hedley Byrne & Co v Heller & Partners Ltd* [1964] AC 465 be treated as a decision establishing a liability 'as if' there had been a contract?
4. Are all pieces of legislation aimed at the same target readers?
5. Is the 'reasonable man' (now 'reasonable person') a fiction? What about the 'implied term' in contract?
6. Can legal reasoning be 'demystified'? (Cf Alexander and Sherwin (2008); Samuel (2009).)
7. What if it transpired that the *Corpus Iuris Civilis* (the great sourcebook of Roman law) was a forgery? The whole collection was a text invented and written by 9th-century clerics working for the papacy. There never were any Roman jurists and there never was a Roman legal literature. Would it matter?

Conclusions

A whole range of questions were posed at the beginning of this book and it would be idle to think that they have all received an adequate response in these chapters. What these chapters have, hopefully, achieved is to set out a number of fruitful approaches or frameworks within which judging and legal reasoning might be understood.

1. *Diachronic framework*. The first of such approaches is this. Judging, and the legal reasoning associated with it, is a phenomenon that is probably best approached, first of all, diachronically: what has legal reasoning been? The obvious starting point is the body of work produced by the Roman jurists, although this might not actually be the most suitable place to begin. It could be argued that the Post-Glossators or Commentators – the late medieval Italian jurists – are the lawyers who developed the techniques that are more directly associated with today's legal profession. They form the link between the old Roman jurists and the modern Western lawyer. From the position of these late medieval jurists one can look backwards to the casuistry of the Romans and then forwards to the axiomatic thinking of, if not actually today's jurists, the German legal scientists of the 19th century (see generally Gordley, 2013). What the Post-Glossators achieved was a clear shift of emphasis from a remedies model of reasoning (see 3.5) to one where law was seen as a matter of rules (see 2.1) and interpretation (see 2.3). This is not to suggest that these jurists abandoned a casuistic approach to law; indeed quite the opposite. But they perfected the dialectical method into one that was virtually algorithmic in its structure. Their commentaries were to be reorganised into coherent and systematised conceptual structures by the schools of jurists who succeeded them. These developments all involved changes in reasoning methods. Induction and analogy ('bottom up') gave way to systemisation and deduction ('top down') (see 1.5).

A diachronic approach – what legal reasoning has been – equally permits one to identify what might be called the institutional focal points around which types of reasoning methods develop. Here Roman law itself proves fundamental in that it contains the foundations not just for all of these different models – the remedies (*actiones*), rule (*regula*), rights (*ius*), interpretation (*interpretatio*) and policy (*utilitas*) approaches are all to be found, with more or less intensity, within the texts of the *Corpus Iuris Civilis* – but for the basic concepts that now dominate all legal thinking. Ownership, possession, contract, fault, obligation and the like are all Roman.

The common law tradition did of course develop independently of Roman law and its subsequent scholarship, but the different models were able to exert their influences through legal science and legal theory. 'Whereas English law has remained relatively free of Roman influences', wrote Peter Stein, 'English jurisprudence has traditionally turned for inspiration to the current continental theories, necessarily based on Roman law' (Stein, 1980, 123). This influence was particularly strong in the 19th century: the great Roman law concepts of ownership, possession, fault and the like 'were borrowed from the civil law in the nineteenth century, and grafted onto the English common law' (Gordley, 2013, 22). This is not to assert that legal reasoning and methods have become one and the same with those of the civil law; the common lawyers were never really seduced by the systemisers and their 'top-down' approach and this is why common law reasoning is often seen as being closer to the methods of the Roman and medieval jurists. Induction and analogy seem to dominate in the judgments more than the syllogism.

2. *Axiomatic and casuistic approaches*. This distinction between a top-down (deductive) and a bottom-up (casuistic) method provides a second fruitful approach, for it is actually of importance in legal reasoning. Take a case like *Blackpool & Fylde Aero Club v Blackpool BC* (see 5.1) where a tender was negligently rejected without proper consideration by a local authority. The tenderer brought an action for damages based on breach of a collateral contract and on the tort of negligence. If one were to take a top-down approach one would start out from two principles seemingly well established by the precedents. A contract to contract is not a contract (*Courtney & Fairbairn v Tolani Brother (Hotels) Ltd* [1975] 1 WLR 297); and no duty of care is owed in respect of pure economic loss (*Spartan Steel & Alloys Ltd v Martin & Co* [1973] 1 QB 27). Applying these principles in a deductive manner to the facts, one could plausibly arrive at the conclusion that the claimant had no case. Yet the claimant was successful because this was not the approach adopted by Bingham LJ who was responsible for the principal judgment in the Court of Appeal. As the extract from his judgment indicates (see 5.1), he starts not from principle, but from within the facts, where he succeeds in transforming a legitimate 'expectation' into an enforceable 'right' without even mentioning any precedent. The law in this case arose 'upwards' from the facts and not 'downwards' from some

axiom. As the medieval jurist Baldus said: '*ius est implicitu facto*' (comment on D.9.2.52.2).

3. *Official and unofficial portraits.* A third fruitful approach to judging and legal reasoning is the metaphorical dichotomy employed by Mitchel Lasser in his work on French law (Lasser, 2004). This is the dichotomy, used as we have seen in this book, between an official and an unofficial portrait of styles and methods of reasoning. The official portrait, as employed in this book, is one that views legal reasoning from a position internal to the discipline of law and thus governed by what has been described as the authority paradigm (see 5.1). It is the view of the judges themselves and of academic commentators and legal theorists writing from an internal position. Such a view can then be contrasted with an unofficial portrait, which adopts a position from outside the discipline of law. How might a social science theorist view the methods of the judges? These two different viewpoints do not necessarily radically diverge; distinctions between different schemes of intelligibility as a means of analysing reasoning (on which see 4.4, 6.2, 6.5 and 6.6) might well find favour with many working within the authority paradigm. But realist theories of law (see 4.1) have attracted considerable hostility from some jurists. 'The realists and post-realists', wrote Peter Birks, 'have done a good job of debunking legal science' (Birks, 1996, 4). Indeed Realism can find itself on occasions in complete conflict with the authority paradigm. To argue, for example, that the true motivation behind a judicial decision is to be found in the political orientation or social conditioning of the various judges cannot form part of an official portrait of judicial reasoning. The ideology of the official portrait is one that sees judges as neutrally applying an objective body of law or laws.

However there are several ways in which Realism can offer more positive contributions to the official portrait. First, the work of feminist jurisprudence writers on legal reasoning ought to serve as a gentle reminder that gender does matter in the world of judging and legal reasoning (see in particular Hunter, McGlynn and Rackley, 2010). Various remarks by Lady Hale confirm this point and given her role as a Supreme Court judge her comments can be said to be at least a part of the official portrait. Secondly, although there is some recognition by the judiciary that the policy model of reasoning can be controversial on occasions given that the judges do not often base their assertions on reliable empirical research, policy reasoning, being functional in its methodological orientation, is nevertheless an aspect of Realism itself. And it cannot be doubted that the policy model is well entrenched in English law. Thirdly, one of the most important contributions of the

American Realists has been with respect to the importance of facts, and how they are (re-)constructed and categorised, in judging and legal reasoning. The extract from Karl Llewellyn remains a classic analysis of this aspect of law (see 4.2).

4. *Facts and image (representation theory).* The emphasis on facts is important for a fourth fruitful approach to judging and legal reasoning. Looking at art and film theory can be valuable because both can offer theories about representation and image (as well as about other aspects of reasoning). In a case like *Re Rowland* (see 4.4) the difference between the dissenting judge and one of the majority judges was a difference between two described hypothetical images regarding speculation on the facts. At what level of observation are facts to be viewed, for different levels give different images? And in *Miller v Jackson* (see 4.2) the majority judges created an unfavourable image of the claimant which enabled them to deny her the remedy she was seeking. Image representation also plays an important role with regard to certain legal concepts – in particular with respect to the corporate legal person whose conceptual 'existence' has been explained by reference to the image of the human body (see 4.6). Image comparison is another reasoning device. In the *Woodland* case (see 4.8) the Court of Appeal compared the facts of the case with a school outing to a zoo and this led them to deny the existence of a non-delegable duty. When the case went to the Supreme Court, Lady Hale suggested a different image in the paragraph where she contrasted three types of school. In highlighting the fact that the first two schools would be liable to a victim in the claimant's position she created an image which indicated how anomalous it would be for the third school to escape liability. The Supreme Court accordingly overturned the Court of Appeal's decision.

Facts, then, do not arrive in some descriptively neutral form. They are organised and categorised so as to be amenable to legal categories, concepts and rules and they may, in addition, as Stephen Waddams observes, be stated at countless different levels of generality (see 4.2). The American Realists, as we have said, started to investigate this aspect of judging and legal reasoning, but subsequent theorists have not really taken the issue much further. Instead the focus has been on rule application and on interpretation of rules and principles (see, for example, a book like Alexander and Sherwin, 2008). Professor Mathieu (see 4.8) has made the point that there is an important difference between what might be called reality (facts) and the representation of this reality (model) and she has used the example of the map to illustrate the point. The map of a landscape is not the landscape itself and should not be confused with it. This is a theme exploited by the film *Vertigo*, which merges *persona* (person represented) with an actual person to such an extent that the two become one and the same, which itself acts as the basis of a disturbing tension (see 4.7) (the recent film *Phoenix* (2014) does much the same). Law finds itself in a similar situation with respect to legal personality: when do real persons (employees) become one and the same as the corporate person (employer) itself? Cases such as *Tesco v Nattrass* (see 4.6) indicate how difficult this issue can be on occasions. Case law suggests that it is answered by image representation: is the employee to be considered as just a 'limb' of the 'body' or its 'directing mind'?

This reference to maps has a wider relevance since maps have been used to explain how reality and knowledge of this reality ought not to be confused. Knowledge models, like maps, give only partial knowledge of what is being modelled since much depends upon the level of observation (see 6.4). Dominique Desjeux himself uses the map to explain this point: a single map cannot give knowledge of the whole detailed landscape. If one wants to reach a specific address in an unfamiliar town many miles away one will need more than one map; one might start with a large-scale motorway map and finish with a street plan (Desjeux, 2004, 12–14). If one is viewing the planet from outer space one sees only forests, but if one is at ground level in the middle of such a forest one sees only trees.

5. *Taxonomy and reasoning*. Peter Birks used this metaphor of the map as a means of modelling law itself. The importance of Justinian's *Institutes* is, he asserted, that it provides an overall map of the law and thus permits one part of the law to 'speak to' another part (see 5.5). At a lower level of abstraction there are of course more detailed categories where indeed such detail may obscure the overall plan. But, according to the late Professor Birks, a knowledge of legal taxonomy is vital to legal science and to legal reasoning if one is to have coherence and stability in the law. What he (and Dr Eric Descheemaeker) saw as intersecting categories have to be avoided because such intersection leads to irrationality in that the law might end up both denying (in one category) and granting (via another category) a remedy with respect to the same set of facts. The map here is being used to counter a realist view of law – that is to say one that judges law in terms of its instrumentalist function – by an appeal to a highly coherent structuralist model, something of course jurists have been trying to achieve since the 16th century (see 1.3–1.4). The image here is one of law as some kind of calculating software that reasons in a similar way as a mathematical calculator (*mos mathematicus*).

This structuralist model – which is usually associated with the rule (see 2.1) and (or) rights (see 3.1) model – stands in contrast to the remedies (cause of action) (see 3.5) and the interest models (see 3.4) of reasoning. These models do not envisage law in terms of a highly coherent conceptual structure. Instead the reasoning consists in matching various causes of action, or identifying particular interests, through an analysis of the facts themselves. One undertakes an analogical comparison between the facts of the litigation dispute and the fact situation envisaged by the cause of action. That one cause of action (for example trespass) may not provide a remedy but another cause of action (say public nuisance) does causes no conceptual crisis (see *Esso v Southport Corporation*, above 3.5). The same is true with regard to the interest model. If the legal conditions are fulfilled with respect to granting a remedy to protect one particular and identifiable interest (say defined economic loss) then the claimant will succeed even if the facts disclose another interest which might not attract a legal remedy (say reputation). This approach was confirmed in *Spring v Guardian Assurance* (see 5.5) and it indicates how reasoning by analogy can lead to different conclusions than reasoning via deduction. Yet does this cause of action and (or) interest approach risk creating a law of categories unable to speak one with another? Certainly this was Professor Birks' view. But of course all the causes of action and interests would all be related, like words in a dictionary, by the alphabet, prompting one to recall a comment by Professor Nicholas Kasirer (now an appeal court judge) that the common law is 'chaos with an index' (Kasirer, 1997). One is back, perhaps, to the distinction between axiomatic and casuistic reasoning (see Jonsen and Toulmin, above 5.1).

6. *Schemes of intelligibility.* Yet summing up legal reasoning in terms of a dichotomy between axiomatic (deductive) and casuistic (inductive and analogical) reasoning is not sufficient to capture the complexities of legal reasoning. How are facts and indeed texts to be 'read'? What are the frameworks used by social scientists when attempting to understand and to describe accurately a particular phenomenon? A fifth fruitful approach to judging and legal reasoning is, accordingly, to examine reasoning through schemes of intelligibility (see Berthelot, above 6.1).

Now lawyers have not traditionally thought about these *grilles de lecture* in any systematic way, although they have been conscious about distinguishing functionalism from structuralism (formalism) and, perhaps, causality from hermeneutics. Thus Professor Birks 'read' law through a stucturalist model while Ronald Dworkin (see 2.5–2.6) read it through a hermeneutical one. The Realists, in contrast to both of these jurists, saw law through a functionalist scheme (Cohen, 1935). Yet these schemes can explain fundamental differences between legal theories and between types of reasoning employed by judges. For example a difference of scheme often explains the divergence between majority and dissenting judges. In *Mirvahedy v Henley* (see 4.4) one of the judges read section 2(2) of the Animals Act from a conceptual structuralist position while one of the dissenting judges approached it through a functionalist scheme. And in *Birmingham CC v Oakley* (see 2.4) one can see how a dialectical scheme was employed by the majority to restrict the scope of the word 'state' by setting up an opposition between 'state' and 'layout'.

Of course merely identifying different schemes is hardly sufficient to explain the complexities of judging and legal reasoning. Each scheme has its own mass of literature in which there are theories, conflicts, debates, analysis and explanations. Causality and hermeneutics, for example, are areas of epistemology and philosophy that would need a lifetime to examine their literary content in all of its rich depth. Given the importance of these two schemes for lawyers – causation being a central concept in the law of obligations both as a question of fact and of law – merely talking in terms of the causal scheme of intelligibility is hardly sufficient. Much the same could be said about hermeneutics. As with causality, the jurist will need to break free of his/her discipline in order to have a full appreciation of the debates and approaches that underpin this scheme of intelligibility. This said, the judges themselves are unlikely for the most part to have an in-depth knowledge of the interdisciplinary literature with respect to the various schemes and so at the level of legal reasoning itself one is unlikely to find any judicial discussion of say Hans Gadamer. The hermeneutical orientation of much legal reasoning is therefore likely to remain at a fairly simplistic level (summed up in a number of authority paradigm approaches such as the literal, golden and mischief rules).

7. *Reception theory.* Nevertheless, those who do have an appreciation of the literature on hermeneutics will be aware that whatever the level of sophistication to be found in the judgments themselves the idea that interpretation is a dialogue between author and reader is of immense importance to jurists. At a basic level many judges are aware that they are addressing (evidently) an audience and that this audience might have an input into the judging and reasoning itself. The primary audience for judges is no doubt the corps of lawyers, these days embracing academics as well as practitioners (which was not always the case in English law). But Lady Hale in *Woodland* (see 2.6) reminds lawyers that the 'man on the Underground' matters as well. Accordingly a sixth fruitful approach

to judging and reasoning in law is reception theory, itself fashioned within film studies.

We have noted that film theorists have identified three categories within this theory, namely text-activated, reader-activated and context-activated orientations (see 6.6). It should immediately be evident that these orientations have relevance for jurists given that the source of law these days is almost uniquely textual, whether statutory or case law (judgments). In the civil law tradition we have seen that whatever the original intention behind the promulgation of a civil code, such codes today cannot be regarded as a matter of text-activated texts. Codes are context-activated in that modern private law is to be seen as a joint exercise between doctrinal writers and the text of the code itself (see Niglia, above 6.6). Indeed some articles such as article 1384 (see now art 1242) of the *Code civil* might even be regarded as reader activated.

In English law, given the constitutional rule of the supremacy of Parliament, one might think that all legislation is primarily text activated. In truth the position is far from simple. Certainly the general rule of statutory interpretation is to give expression to the will of Parliament but this rule is qualified by another norm that such a will is to be found only in the words of the text itself. This means that the judges, as readers, have an input that is by no means negligible. Indeed with regard to human rights, the legislator has deliberately inserted what might be called a reader-activated clause (Human Rights Act 1998 s 3, above 2.4). A similar attitude applies to contractual texts. The intention of the parties is to be found in the words of the contract itself and thus when it comes to interpretation it certainly is not possible to assert that the approach is text activated in the sense that one is giving expression to the actual intention of the parties. Recourse might well be made to the reasonable business person in order to avoid an absurd result and this surely represents something of a context-activated approach.

Reception theory will, again, not act in itself as a framework capable of explaining the detailed complexities of legal reasoning. What it can do is to focus on the relationship between the author of a text and the reader or audience at whom the text is directed. Legal texts can differ in their target audience or reader; the French *Code civil* was aimed at the population in general while the German Civil Code (*Bürgerliches Gesetzbuch*) employed a language and set of concepts that could only be understood by jurists formed within the Pandectist tradition (Zweigert and Kötz, 1998, 144). English statutes do not on the whole seem to have the general population as their target readers – although there may be exceptions such as the Theft Act 1968 – and many in fact cannot be understood unless one has had a common law training. For example, to understand section 2(1) of the Misrepresentation Act 1967 one needs to have a good knowledge of the tort of deceit. However, given the history of the relationship between the English judges and legislation it would be difficult to state that there has traditionally been a partnership between author and reader and this is one reason why English statutes are detailed and often opaque. They are designed largely as text-activated documents. Perhaps things are changing. Moreover a perfectly respectable argument can be advanced that a reader-activated response would be inappropriate in respect of some legislative provisions which proved controversial at their drafting stage and which provoked intense political debate. It is not the role of the judiciary to reopen these debates. In short, reception theory permits one to escape from the idea that there is a particular type of reasoning associated with, say, the interpretation of statutes. Whatever lawyers and judges might state, the interpretation model (see 2.3) should perhaps always be considered in terms of the target readers and the input, as it affects reasoning, that such readers will bring to the text. Much no doubt depends upon the text itself and whether it is a kind of text that can be classed within one of the three orientations identified by film theorists.

8. *Restating legal reasoning*. So can legal reasoning be restated in any epistemologically satisfactory way? Legal writers who have turned their attention to legal reasoning have on the whole tended to adopt one of two approaches. Either they have, particularly in general books on a legal system, adopted a viewpoint internal to the discipline of law (authority paradigm) or they have asserted a prescriptive theory about how judges ought to reason. These approaches are perfectly respectable, but they often fail to give a full epistemological account of how judges reason. The official portraits tend, for example, to focus on what might be termed symbolic knowledge (language and numbers) and they ignore the role of non-symbolic knowledge, for example the use of imagery to create impressions (see 4.5). There are exceptions to this generality; there is work on the use of analogy and metaphors which might be said to rely more on non-symbolic knowledge. But of course it is very difficult to fashion a prescriptive theory using non-symbolic knowledge. Indeed it is very difficult actually to fashion a convincing prescriptive theory about legal reasoning because of the diversity of reasoning possibilities open to judges (induction, deduction, analogy, schemes of intelligibility, metaphors, fact construction and so on). Another difficulty is that legal reasoning is not like, say, medical reasoning where a medic's diagnosis will in the end be tested by the facts (Samuel, 2015). Legal conclusions are not open to falsification, although they are open of course to criticism. The only epistemological restraint is consensus; a judge who

uses inappropriate reasoning will be censured by other judges and (or) by the wider legal community.

The result is that gaining knowledge about legal reasoning is dependent upon the models one cares to employ, for different models give different forms of knowledge. Social science epistemologists have long known this, but perhaps it is the authority paradigm that has tended to restrict the juristic vision. One should not be surprised because the authority paradigm is itself determined by an ideological vision in which judges should be neutral in the application of the law. They should – at least according to the traditional civilian view – be more like computers. And computers 'reason' using only symbolic knowledge, all non-symbolic knowledge being regarded as emotional or biased and therefore unsuitable within the official portrait of legal reasoning.

If, then, legal reasoning is to be restated in terms of its epistemological foundations, venturing beyond the official portrait is vital. Hopefully these chapters have started to do just this. But if there is one lesson to be retained it is this. There are, as we have said, a variety of different knowledge models operating at different levels and taking different objects as their point of focus. Each of these different models is, usually, perfectly respectable in its own right; but the knowledge revealed by each is likely to be different. Which model dominates at any one moment will not be a matter either of correspondence or of the reliability of its coherence structure; it will be a matter of consent among those who make up the discipline of law.

Bibliography

Alexander, L and Sherwin, E (2008), *Demystifying Legal Reasoning* (Cambridge University Press)
Ariely, D (2008), *Predictably Irrational* (Harper)
Atias, C (1994), *Épistémologie du droit* (Presses Universitaires de France)
Atiyah, PS and Summers, RS (1987), *Form and Substance in Anglo-American Law* (Oxford University Press)
Baker, J (2002), *An Introduction to English Legal History* (Butterworths, 4th ed)
Baker, J (2003), *The Oxford History of the Laws of England: Volume VI 1483–1558* (Oxford University Press)
Barr, C (2002), *Vertigo* (British Film Institute Publishing)
Bell, J (1983), *Policy Arguments in Judicial Decisions* (Oxford University Press)
Bergel, J-L (2012), *Théorie générale du droit* (Dalloz, 5th ed)
Berman, H (1983), *Law and Revolution: The Formation of the Western Legal Tradition* (Harvard University Press)
Birks, P (1996), Equity in the Modern Law: An Exercise in Taxonomy 26 *University of Western Australia Law Review* 1
Birks, P (ed) (1997), *The Classification of Obligations* (Oxford University Press)
Bouriau, C (2013), *Le 'comme si': Kant, Vaihinger et le fictionalisme* (Les Éditions du Cerf)
Cohen, F (1935), Transcendental Nonsense and the Functional Approach 35 *Columbia Law Review* 809
Conte, C (2015), From Only the Bottom Up? Legitimate Forms of Judicial Reasoning in Private Law 35 *Oxford Journal of Legal Studies* 1
Dawkins, R and Coyne, J, 'One Side Can be Wrong', *The Guardian*, 1 September 2005
Del Mar, M and Twining, W (eds) (2015), *Legal Fiction in Theory and Practice* (Springer)
Desjeux, D (2004), *Les sciences sociales* (Presses Universitaires de France)
Durgnat, R (1967), *Films and Feelings* (Faber & Faber)

Duxbury, N (2013), *Elements of Legislation* (Cambridge University Press)

Dworkin, R (1986), *Law's Empire* (Fontana)

Gordley, J (2013), *The Jurists: A Critical History* (Oxford University Press)

Gray, K and Gray, S (2003), The Rhetoric of Reality, in J Getzler (ed), *Rationalizing Property, Equity and Trusts* (Butterworths) 204

Griffith, J (1997), *The Politics of the Judiciary* (Fontana, 5th ed)

Hohfeld, W (1919), *Fundamental Legal Conceptions* (Yale University Press; reprint, 1966)

Hunter, R, McGlynn, C and Rackley, E (2010), *Feminist Judgments: From Theory to Practice* (Hart)

Ibbetson, D (1999), *A Historical Introduction to the Law of Obligations* (Oxford University Press)

Johnston, D (ed) (2015), *The Cambridge Companion to Roman Law* (Cambridge University Press)

Jolowicz, H (1957), *Roman Foundations of Modern Law* (Oxford University Press)

Jones, JW (1940), *Historical Introduction to the Theory of Law* (Oxford University Press)

Jouanjan, O (2005), *Une histoire de la pensée juridique en Allemagne (1800–1918)* (Presses Universitaires de France)

Kasirer, N (1997), 'K' as a Structure of Anglo-American Legal Knowledge 22 *Canadian Law Libraries* 159

Lasser, M (2004), *Judicial Deliberations: A Comparative Analysis of Judicial Transparency and Legitimacy* (Oxford University Press)

Lawson, F (1980), *Remedies of English Law* (Butterworths, 2nd ed)

Lobban, M (1991), *The Common Law and English Jurisprudence 1760–1850* (Oxford University Press)

MacCormick, N (1978), *Legal Reasoning and Legal Theory* (Oxford University Press)

MacCormick, N (2005), *Rhetoric and the Rule of Law: A Theory of Legal Reasoning* (Oxford University Press)

Maclean, I (1992), *Interpretation and Meaning in the Renaissance* (Cambridge University Press)

Maine, H (1890), *Early Law and Custom* (John Murray)

Milsom, S (1981), *Historical Foundations of the Common Law* (Butterworths, 2nd ed)

Ost, F (1990), *Droit et intérêt: volume 2: Entre droit et non-droit: l'intérêt* (Facultés universitaires Saint-Louis, Brussels)

Samuel, G (2000), Can Gaius Really be Compared to Darwin? 49 *International & Comparative Law Quarterly* 297

Samuel, G (2003), *Epistemology and Method in Law* (Ashgate)

Samuel, G (2004), English Private Law: Old and New Thinking in the Taxonomy Debate 24 *Oxford Journal of Legal Studies* 335
Samuel, G (2005), Can the Common Law Be Mapped? 55 *University of Toronto Law Journal* 271
Samuel, G (2008), Is Law Really a Social Science? A View from Comparative Law 67 *Cambridge Law Journal* 288
Samuel, G (2009), Can Legal Reasoning Be Demystified? 29 *Legal Studies* 181
Samuel, G (2013), *A Short Introduction to the Common Law* (Edward Elgar)
Samuel, G (2014), *An Introduction to Comparative Law Theory and Method* (Hart)
Samuel, G (2015), Is Legal Reasoning Like Medical Reasoning? 34 *Legal Studies* 323
Staiger, J (1992), *Interpreting Films: Studies in the Historical Reception of American Cinema* (Princeton University Press)
Stein, P (1980), *Legal Evolution: The Story of an Idea* (Cambridge University Press)
Stein, P (1999), *Roman Law in European History* (Cambridge University Press)
Twining, W (1985), *Karl Llewellyn and the Realist Movement* (Weidenfeld & Nicolson, reprint 1985)
Twining, W and Miers, D (2010), *How To Do Things With Rules* (Cambridge University Press, 5th ed)
Waddams, S (2003), *Dimensions of Private Law: Categories and Concepts in Anglo-American Legal Reasoning* (Cambridge University Press)
Waddams, S (2011), *Principle and Policy in Contract Law: Competing or Complementary Concepts?* (Cambridge University Press)
Weir, T (2005), Recent Developments in Causation in English Tort Law, in B Fauvarque-Cosson, E Picard and A Voinnesson (eds), *De tous horizons: Mélanges Xavier Blanc Jouvan* (Société de Législation Comparée) 883
Zakrzewski, R (2005), *Remedies Reclassified* (Oxford University Press)
Zimmermann, R (1996), *The Law of Obligations* (Oxford University Press)
Zweigert, K and Kötz, H (1998), *An Introduction to Comparative Law* (Oxford University Press, 3rd ed, trans T Weir)

Index